The Jews of Lemberg

The Jews of Lemberg

A Journey to Empty Places

Heleen Zorgdrager
Michiel Driebergen

VALLENTINE MITCHELL
LONDON • CHICAGO, IL

First published in 2017 by Vallentine Mitchell

Catalyst House,
720 Centennial Court, Centennial Park,
Elstree WD6 3SY, UK

Independent Publishers Group
814 N Franklin St, Chicago, IL
60610, USA

www.vmbooks.com

Original Dutch title De Joden van Lemberg, een reis naar lege plekken

Design: Diderik Prak
Maps: Herman Zonderland

British Library Cataloguing in Publication Data:
An entry can be found on request

ISBN 978 1 910383 27 8 (cloth)
ISBN 978 1 910383 23 0 (paper)
ISBN 978 1 910383 24 7 (ebook)

Library of Congress Cataloging in Publication Data
An entry can be found on request

Printed by Independent Publishers Group, Chicago

The authors dedicate this book to Sharona, Boris and Siva, with both gratitude and respect for their precious life stories.

Image credits

Photos of present-day Lviv: Diderik Prak (www.dehondsrugpers.nl), Grigoriy Prystay and Hans Bijzet (www.hans-bijzet.nl).

The map of the ghetto on page 79 was kindly made available by the United States Holocaust Memorial Museum in Washington, D.C. (www.ushmm.org).

The photo of the Great Suburban Synagogue on pages 68 and 69 was sourced from the book *Lemberg - Lwów - Lviv: Album 1880-1919*, by Claudia Erdheim and was made available by Album Verlag für Photographie in Vienna. The destroyed synagogue was photographed by Joe J. Heydecker (1916-1997).

Several historical images were provided by the Center for Urban History of East Central Europe in Lviv (www.lvivcenter.org).

Most of the other historical pictures were found on the Internet. It was not always possible to locate the relevant copyright holders. If there are any persons or authorities who may be legitimate copyright holders of one or more photos in this text, please contact the publisher.

Contents

Prologue

You could easily pass it by… in the middle of the historical heart of the city of Lviv, between museums and medieval facades, lies a vacant lot surrounded by a corrugated-iron fence. There is garbage; rampant shrubs, overgrown ruins and the homeless seek refuge there. There is no longer any indication that the Golden Rose Synagogue, once one of the oldest and most famous places of worship in Europe, used to be here. Such was the situation until 2016. Our story about the Jews of Lviv (Lemberg) began to revolve around this strange, empty spot. We found many more of these empty spaces: squares, markets and patches of green wedged between prewar premises. They are now used as children's playgrounds, as small markets for selling fresh fruit, or as parking spots.

At one time, multicultural Lemberg had forty-five Jewish synagogues and houses of worship. During the Holocaust, almost all the Jewish inhabitants of Lviv were murdered and the synagogues, save for two, razed to the ground. "Lemberik," as the Jews called the city, was once a center of Chassidic Judaism, the Yiddish language and its culture. Sholem Aleichem lived here, as did the young Martin Buber and the poetess Dvoyre Fogel. Once this city was the lifeblood of Jewish Galicia with its shtetls, its melancholic klezmer music and its colorful folk tales.

A modern-day visitor to Lviv with even the slightest inkling of the rich Jewish past of this city may feel somewhat inconvenienced upon arrival. Here you are in this stunningly beautiful yet nowadays also very Ukrainian city center. Where can traces of that Jewish past be found? Nowhere in the city will you come across signs that point you toward the important "Jewish" sites. Even travel guides reveal little of the Jewish history of Lviv.

We were those inconvenienced travelers when we visited Lviv for the first time. We went looking for that past. We found sources: historical information, stories, places, photos and, above all, people who unlocked for us the history of the Jews in the city. What is the story behind the empty places? Are there still any material remainders of the past? Surprisingly, there are a lot. In fact, apart from the houses of prayer, the majority of the heritage of the Jewish inhabitants remains upright. Gymnasia (high schools), theaters and merchant buildings are even being used, albeit with a different designation. Blocks of houses from the ghetto of World War II are there as well, as is the former forced-labor camp.

We were not only driven by an interest in the past; we also wanted to tell the story of the Jews who live in Lviv now. Are there any? How do they live in this post-Soviet city? Where do their roots lie? How did they rebuild the Jewish community life against the dark background of the Holocaust?

We would like to pass on these stories to people who, just like us, wish to immerse themselves in Lviv's past and present from a near distance. This will bring them closer either in their imaginations, or - why not? - in reality, when they travel to the city with this book in their backpack, to be used as a travel guide.

During our search, we employ the life stories of three survivors as a starting point. To begin our journey, we meet the very last Yiddish-speaking inhabitant of the city, who remains committed to both his language and culture. Next, we encounter the rabbi of Lviv, who finds a way of dealing with the past. To conclude, we speak extensively with one of the few survivors of the Holocaust, a strong woman who lives in Jerusalem.

Connecting their narratives through descriptions of the places in the city that play or played a role in their life stories, we reveal the most interesting locations and tales that stir our emotions, even today. Every chapter contains notes that will guide you to these areas, as well as other practical information. At the end of the book, you will find an acknowledgement of literary sources, plus additional reading material.

Meanwhile, we both know Lviv well, albeit from different perspectives. Heleen Zorgdrager is Associate Professor of Ecumenical Theology at the Ukrainian Catholic University in Lviv. She joins in the efforts of bridging the gaps between churches and religious groups in Ukraine.

Michiel Driebergen is a journalist and correspondent, covering Lviv and Cracow (Poland) for Dutch media. He tries to align the multicultural history of Lemberg with the Europe of today.

We would like to thank the colleagues of the Ukrainian Catholic University in Lviv for their invaluable information and interaction. We especially want to mention Myroslav Marynovych, one of the pioneers of the Ukrainian-Jewish dialogue since the 1990s, Dr. Yaroslav Hrytsak, Professor of Modern History, and Oksana Sikorska, a history student who is especially dedicated to Ukrainian-Jewish relations.

Dr. Sofia Dyak, Director of the Center for Urban History of East Central Europe in Lviv, stimulated us with her expert advice and warm interest in this project. Iryna Kotlobulatova, researcher at the Center for Urban

History, helped us to find unique pictorial material and to make it available to us. Marco Carynnyk, writer, editor, and historical researcher, generously shared his knowledge of Soviet and German politics in Ukraine in the 1930s and 1940s, and Polish-Jewish-Ukrainian relations with us. He was of great value in improving the historical and stylistic quality of the text. The cooperation of Diderik Prak, literary scholar and publisher, turned out to be invaluable in the realization of this book. He only knew Lemberg and Galicia from Central-European literature; however, in 2011 he visited the city for the first time and was immediately captivated by it. We are grateful for his assistance in the final editing and design processes, and for his infectious enthusiasm for Habsburg culture and Jewish life in Central Europe.

Thanks to the dedicated work of translation by Jantine van der Knaap and Kristie Szalanski, this book, originally published in Dutch, is now available to a wider readership.

We thank Herman Zonderland who prepared the map of Jewish sites referred to in the book, and Marie Christine Hansen-Couturier who was of great help in making the index.

Special thanks go to the Ukrainian Jewish Encounter (UJE, Mississauga, Canada) and to the Friends of Lviv (The Netherlands) for their generous support to this publication.

Without Dr. Sharona Igra-Komem, Boris Dorfman and Rabbi Siva Fainerman, who shared their precious life stories with us, the completion of this book would not have been possible. We dedicate this book to them, with our gratitude and respect.

Michiel Driebergen
Heleen Zorgdrager

Looking for Lemberik

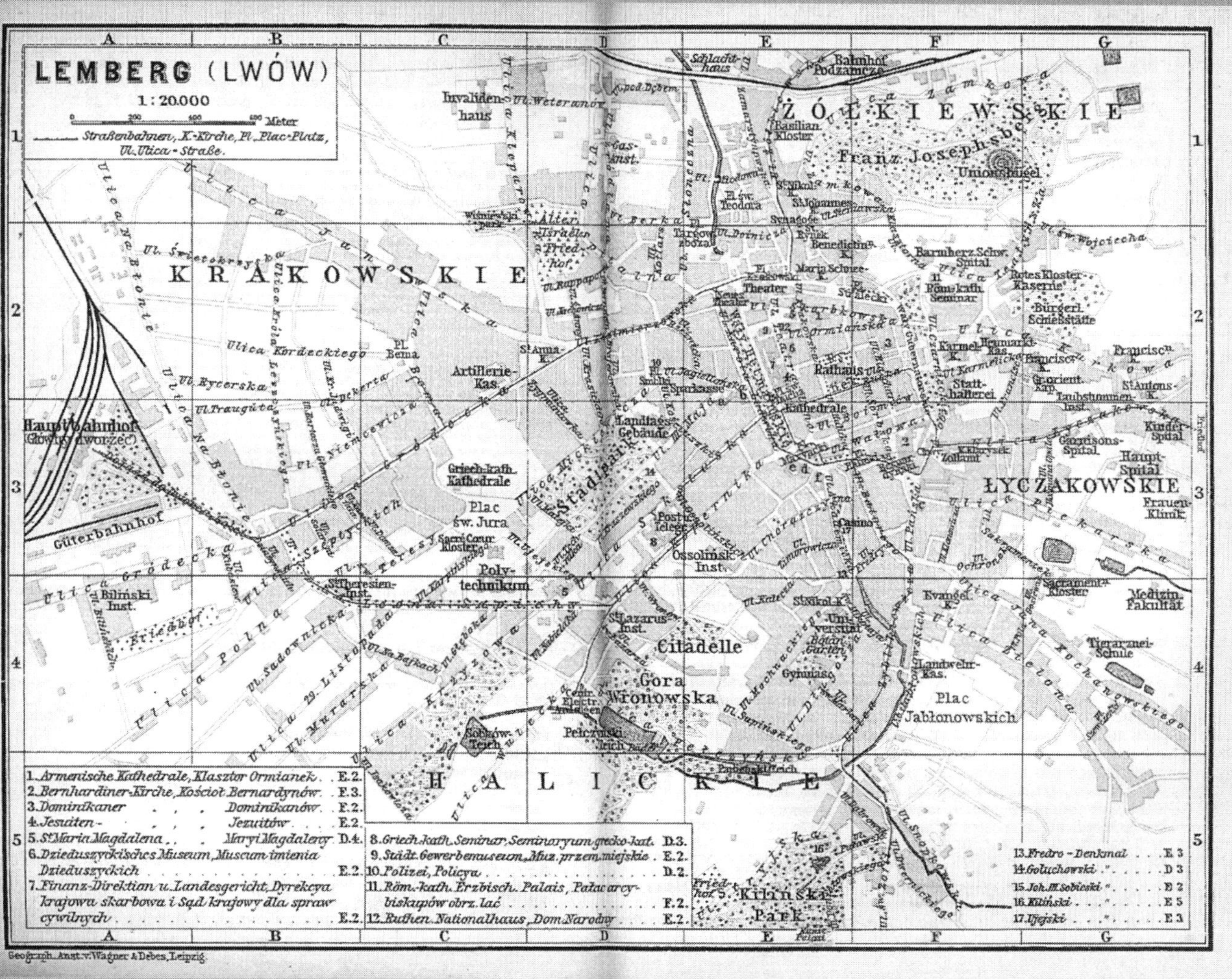

Street plan of Lemberg in the Baedeker Travel Guide, early 20th Century

Looking for Lemberik

Lviv is a wonderful city in which to stroll about. The pavement warms your feet; the clip-clop of horses' hooves echoes throughout the Boulevard of Freedom. Carriages pull lazy tourists across the cobblestones. The tram tinkles cheerfully and impatiently; you cross the street and see girls in sexy high heels sauntering beneath the statue of Shevchenko. On benches, in the shade of the chestnut trees, old men try to beat each other at chess.

The sun lights up the Opera House like a Viennese diamond. People pose in front of the splashing fountain. The sounds of cheerfully shouted orders, friendly greetings and click of camera shutters fill the air. Toddlers circle in little toy cars as their parents dash after them.

As you inhale, the air delivers traces of well-known aromas: coffee, cotton candy and freshly-baked rolls. Scanning the characteristic European facades, Gothic and Baroque architecture, Classicism and Jugendstil are all abundantly represented. In the distance, you catch a glimpse of the mighty castle hill that stands guard over the city.

The medieval city square lies just a stone's throw away – a friendly and cozy place, with its central-European merchant houses, outdoor cafes and nostalgic streetlights. Local youths play in the pond at the feet of Goddess Diana, looking for coins thrown in for good luck by passing travelers.

In the surrounding streets, cathedrals and churches either boast exuberant Catholic towers or offer more sober Protestant brickwork. The narrow streets and courtyards would have you believe that Paris or Prague is not far off.

And yet, you have your suspicions – first impressions still implanted firmly in your mind – since the city had initially welcomed you with its extensive suburbs, evocative of the drab, large-scale high-rise blocks of the Soviet Union. Next to shining BMWs and Kias, decrepit Ladas and Volgas struggle over the lopsided brick roads. Yellow minibuses, known as marshrutkas, are jam-packed, as for many people a car is too costly a possession.

Many monumental buildings look a bit dilapidated, as if Father Time had been given the opportunity to pulverize some European heritage. Colors have faded to pastels; paint is flaking off of the walls. Signage and street names make you reach desperately for a dictionary: Ah, the alienating effect of the Cyrillic script! You glance at your watch and notice that the clock in

A summer's evening on the Boulevard of Freedom, Prospekt Svobody

Lviv is set an hour ahead of Western Europe, adopting the time zone of Kyiv and Minsk.

Although Lviv has almost a million inhabitants and its buildings offer a certain big-city allure, it is obvious that it is a provincial town at heart. In the early evening, when the sun disappears behind the towers of the Elisabeth Cathedral at the end of Doroshenka Street, large groups of elderly people gather at Prospekt Svobody and begin to sing. The strains of Ukrainian folk songs revive the air of country life: a solidarity with the earth and unremitting labor. The elders appear slightly rustic, dressed in traditional garb, with protruding cheekbones and jaw lines resulting in notably angular faces.

Old women sit upon low stools in the marketplace, heads covered and dressed in floral dresses, selling vegetables, eggs, cheese and fresh cow's milk. The typical Russian severity of civil servants behind the service desk is nowhere to be found. In fact, it is possible to perceive a slight insecurity, as foreign languages are not traditionally learned by locals.

The rusting tram rails and broken pavement lying in disrepair imply that the "big money" is being spent elsewhere – somewhere far-off, in a distant capital hundreds of kilometers to the east.

The remains of former glory in the heart of the city

Unknown in the west

However, after you cross the old town center, one thing will immediately win you over: the uniqueness of Lviv. Whereas some historic city centers – such as those of Warsaw, Minsk and Kyiv – were practically wiped off the face of the earth, the center of Lviv remained surprisingly intact. It is, therefore, no accident that the entire city center is proudly inscribed upon UNESCO's World Heritage List.

Those familiar with the tragedy that occurred here in the last century would be even more amazed. The churches, plazas, museums and cemeteries serve as testimony to a rich, multicultural Habsburg city that provided opportunities to a mélange of cultures, religions and influences. Behind the splendid facades lies a wealth of narratives and histories that remain undiscovered.

Very few people have ever heard of Lviv, unless they noticed news reports about the Orange Revolution of 2004. The city became known as the birthplace of that revolution, a non-violent uprising that resulted in a (provisional) government that focused, for the first time, upon nearby Europe instead of far-away Moscow. Nowhere in Ukraine is the mentality more Western than in Lviv. In November 2013, the city was again the cradle of a large protest movement that became known as the Euromaidan revolution. The people's uprising resulted in the establishment of a pro-European government. After Russia annexed Crimea, during the spring of 2014, and after a non-declared war broke out in Eastern Ukraine, the future of Ukraine and Lviv is again threatened.

The very name of the city causes confusion. There is a variety of names used simultaneously. The Latin name for Lviv was Leopolis, meaning "city of lions." Internationally, Lviv is still known as Lvov, the name used during Soviet times. Elderly Dutch and German people may have learned in their geography classes the name Lemberg, which is reminiscent of the Austro-Hungarian Empire. In the 1920s and 1930s, when the city was part of Poland, Germans still called it Lemberg and Poles Lwów, but Ukrainians called it Lviv. During the German occupation, Germans used the name Lemberg, but Poles and Ukrainians still called it Lwów or Lviv. The Yiddish-speaking Jews called the city Lemberik. Present-day inhabitants, depending on the language they are speaking or writing, still call it Lviv, Lwów, or Lvov. On road signs in Ukraine one will just see the name Lviv (Львів).

Book market behind the Dominican Church, featuring the statue of sixteenth-century Ivan Fedoriv (Fyodorov), the first printer in Lemberg

The history of Lviv

The influence of the Habsburg Empire is emphasized by the architecture of Lviv. After the partitioning of Poland in the eighteenth century, Lemberg came under Viennese rule, as the capital of the outlying Austrian province of Galicia. Lemberg and the Polish city of Kraków were sister cities for a long time – two cities with much in common that increasingly resembled one another. A Polish-speaking governing body ruled on behalf of the emperor. Lviv was growing and prospering; architects and city planners came from Vienna to embellish the city. The famous Opera House, constructed at the end of the eighteenth century, is symbolic of this period.

After the Polish general Piłsudski brutally suppressed rising Ukrainian nationalism in the war of 1918–1919, the city was, between the two world wars, part a reborn nationalistic Poland. Snapshots of pre-war Polish Lwów can be seen on old postcards for sale at the book market, and old Polish advertisements are still visible on many housefronts.

Before World War II, Poles comprised about two-thirds of the city's population. After being successively occupied by Russian, German and yet

Józef Piłsudski (1867-1935), liberator of Poland in 1918 and founder of the Second Polish Republic

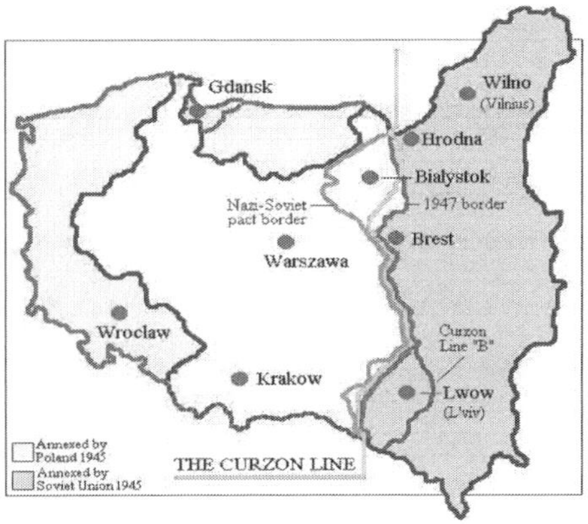

The Curzon Line was a demarcation line from 1919 to 1920 between the Second Polish Republic and Bolshevik Russia, which approximately correlates with the current eastern border of Poland.

again Russian troops, they had to leave their houses in a hurry after the war. The world leaders had decided in Yalta and Potsdam to move Poland's borders several hundred miles westward, to the benefit of the conquering Soviet Union and at the expense of the losing country Germany.

Poland lost its territories in the east and was compensated by receiving areas in what is now the west of Poland. Lviv is still called Lwów in Poland and many Poles feel nostalgic for their native soil. By far, most of the tourists whom you encounter here are Polish, often descendants of the original population. They come in large numbers to visit the city on weekends.

For centuries, the Germans also constituted an important core in Central and Eastern Europe, as they did in Lemberg, which is how the Germans refer to the city. There was an important Lutheran community with a large church. A lot of German was spoken, also by the many Jewish inhabitants of the city. However, after World War II, the Russian victors branded the German inhabitants as potential traitors and, above all, as losers and sent them off to their Heimat, or home country, as Vertriebenen (expellees).

In the Soviet era the Russians dominated every aspect of life; this was a time from which visible traces still remain. The gigantic suburbs of the city were built in the typical style, which you will also find in other former Eastern Bloc countries: gray high-rise buildings - Plattenbau in German - with a Russian-looking street layout. Russian became a compulsory subject at school, and even now almost all of the inhabitants of Lviv aged thirty years and older have command of the language. However, fewer and fewer young people actually speak it these days.

As is customary in a Central European city, the Armenians were also represented to a large degree. Still visible are the traces of the Armenian diaspora, particularly within the famous Armenian Church in the heart of the medieval city center – by far the oldest cathedral in town, surrounded by ancient gravestones.

Today, a vast majority of the population is Ukrainian. They were always modestly, yet obviously, present in the streets, churches and university lecture halls. The ancestors of most of these Ukrainians, though, lived in the surrounding countryside or arrived in the city from eastern regions after World War II. After the expulsion of the Poles and Germans – and the eradication of the Jews – Lviv was virtually an empty city. Displaced people were then able to find a new home here. Visitors are fascinated by the fact that the history of the city was rewritten some seventy years ago; Lviv is an open-air museum of Europe's past. This spectacle of architecture depicts Europe from before the world wars. Lviv is like the décor from a theater that was left behind, the original actors having disappeared.

Commemoration of the Russian and German occupation during World War II at the monument to Shevchenko

Ukrainian nationalism

Like many states in the eastern half of Europe, Ukraine has been independent for only a little over twenty years. In the previous centuries, it was part of the Russian tsarist empire and after World War I, of the Soviet Union. Saint Petersburg – and later, Moscow – suppressed the pursuit of its identity in a vigorous and often relentless way. Over the course of the nineteenth century, a sense of nationality developed; the same happened in the regions of the Habsburg and Ottoman empires. Taras Shevchenko played an important role in the growth of national consciousness for Ukraine. The son of a serf, Shevchenko had been given the opportunity by his father's lord to attend school and study to become an artist. He achieved fame not only for his art and poetry, but for his uncompromising aspiration to emancipate the Ukrainian language and culture. To achieve that goal, he even spent ten years in prison. In Ukraine, Shevchenko is considered the father of the nation and his monument in Lviv – on the gigantic scale that the former Eastern Bloc countries seem to cherish – stands in the heart of the city on the Prospekt Svobody. Other Ukrainian literati, such as Ivan Franko and the poetess Lesya Ukrainka (Larysa Kosach-Kvitka), are also honored in this way.

Ukrainians are still emerging from age-long oppression and bloody persecution. Nationalism is being vigorously promoted by the government, as happens everywhere in the young states of Eastern Europe. The Ukrainian flag, with its sky blue and maize yellow, flutters atop every government building. Every June the German invasion of 1941 is commemorated with patriotic speeches and songs at the monument to Shevchenko. These commemorative events still seem to have the character of a political demonstration, banners emblazoned with slogans against communism and fascism. The persecution and extermination of the Jews of Lviv play no role at all in this commemoration. This has to do, at least in part, with the recollection of the catastrophic history of the Ukrainians themselves; it also reveals traces of their earlier anti-Semitism, which these days appears to have turned into indifference. It looks as if the Jews have disappeared from the collective memory of the people of Lviv.

The Jews of Lemberg

Old image of the Tempel Synagogue on Staryi Rynok

Street scene from around 1900

As befits any multicultural European city from a bygone era, various cultures, religions, languages and traditions coexisted for centuries – for better or for worse. There was a time when borders between countries were less fixed than today. For centuries, periods of great mutual rivalry and of freedom and prosperity have been alternating. If you must choose one group as a symbol of the multicolored history of the city – and simultaneously of its dramatic decline – it should be the Jews.

Jewish culture was of the utmost importance in the development of the city and its surroundings. But those who know anything about the history of this part of Europe will be aware that this culture has virtually disappeared, in a bloody way. And if somebody does remember the name Lemberg, it would be because of the Jews. Perhaps people think of the Chassidic narratives, of Yiddish-speaking Eastern Europe or of the richness of the Galician Jewish culture. This knowledge is often combined with stories about extermination camps, the General Government and the destructive war between the Russians and the Germans. Is there anything left of the old Lemberg? Can anything be found of that Jewish culture in this formerly Soviet city?

If you know where to look, much remains to be seen of the large Jewish influence upon the city, and there is especially a lot to rediscover. Because the people who now inhabit these houses have more important things on their minds than that distant past, which they do not always regard as their own history. A lot of Ukrainians put all of their energy into the toilsome existence of everyday life. For many of them, the prewar history is unfamiliar; their grandparents mostly come from elsewhere.

What is left of the Jewish culture?

The search for the Jewish heritage can make a person feel dispirited. It is for good reason that the subtitle of this book reads "A journey to empty places." Since the old city center is relatively intact, these empty places are conspicuous. In fact, it is mainly the Jewish houses of prayer that have disappeared from the old center. The gaping wounds in the street scene show you how a fabulously wealthy and centuries-old culture was almost completely decimated in a period of just a few months.

However, anyone looking further will discover an impressive Jewish heritage in the buildings of Lviv. Former schools and department stores, theaters and newspaper offices, museums and orphanages – these are "silent witnesses" to an extensive culture. Most of these buildings are still in use, although mostly for a different purpose. Moreover, there has certainly been some "resurrection" of Jewish life in Lviv, if only on a very small scale.

Do not expect any signs pointing visitors towards the Jewish heritage. Most of the travel guides also fail to provide any information about the Jewish past. Visitors themselves will have to take the initiative and explore the city. However, with a little effort, they may experience the invaluable importance Judaism holds within this city.

Street scenes from around 1900

Multicultural Lemberg

What we would like to demonstrate is how the old multicultural Europe remains preserved within the buildings, mentality and various ethnic groups of this area. All cultures mentioned are still present in the city today, albeit in decimated form: as survivors, returnees or newcomers.

However, it is best not to romanticize the former multicultural character of the city. There is much debate about how the various populations coexisted. In prewar Lemberg, the ethnic groups created or found their identity through relating with each other. Every group can be divided into dozens of subgroups and a cultural unit can be split up again into differing religious beliefs or convictions.

Thus, one Jewish inhabitant could completely assimilate into the Polish language and culture, while another would find his identity in the Yiddish language or in a secluded Chassidic lifestyle. The populations commingled – even the Jewish ghetto in the old city center was not exclusively a Jewish quarter. Our search also regularly led us down the wrong track; perhaps it is precisely this kind of confusion that is typical of the multicultural concept.

The Jews of Lemberg. We describe a history that frightens, yet also fascinates, and succinctly explains the history of a large portion of Europe.

History of the Jews of Lemberg

The first Jews arrived in Lemberg in the thirteenth century. By around 1270, a large Jewish community had already lived in the realm of the Kyivan Rus', which extended from far in the east all the way to Galicia–Volhynia, with Kyiv as its radiant center. Lemberg was an attractive city in which Jews, Greeks and Armenians could all settle. Many important trade routes passed this city in the foothills, on the banks of the Poltva River. That is why the first Jews in the city earned a substantial part of their living through trade and financial transactions.

From an old family photo album

In Lemberg, the Jews lived mainly in the Kraków suburb, around Staryi Rynok. After 1350 the Jewish community was divided into two parts. The richer Jews moved to the walled city center; the poorer ones stayed in the suburbs. Both parts had their own government, synagogues and schools, plus separate rights and privileges. From the nineteenth century onwards the Jews also settled - many as well-to-do citizens - outside of these two city districts, in the spacious ring around the center of town. In addition, because the Jews remained a relatively self-sufficient group, tensions with other ethnic communities regularly arose. However, over the centuries, there are also many examples of Jews who – together with Poles and Germans – defended the city against the Tatars or Cossacks.

Emperor Franz Joseph I (1830-1916)

As crown land, the province of Galicia became a part of the Habsburg Dual Monarchy in the eighteenth century, with Lemberg as its capital. The Austrians levied high taxes upon the Jewish population, stimulated assimilation and tried to temper the growth of the community. Some right-wing political parties vigorously stirred up anti-Semitism. However, the Jews found a patron and protector in the emperor. Franz Joseph affectionately referred to them as "my Jews" and ensured that nobody harmed them. The Jews were therefore very favorably disposed towards the emperor and the rich Jewish bankers supported the k.u.k. or königliche und kaiserliche (royal and imperial) politics – specifically, warfare – with large sums of money. The Jews maintained their pivotal economic role and the community grew, not only in numbers but also in diversity.

With regards to the subject of religion, there were three main movements: Chassidic, Orthodox and Progressive Judaism. The biggest persuasion in Eastern Europe, as well as in Lemberg, was Chassidism. Poor people generally belonged to the Chassidim. They were proud of their Judaism, with a lifestyle of simplicity, piety, cheerfulness and brotherly love. The differences between the movements meant that there was always a lot of "life" in the community – heated debates between rabbis and Talmudists. At the end of the nineteenth century, a Zionist movement was also founded.

The Jewish inhabitants lived in Lemberg as they did within the smaller towns of the countryside: in their shtetl, their own community. In the walled center of the city they had their own quarter, just like the Armenians. If you walk through these streets, have a good look through the gates inside and discover the courtyards with their surrounding balustrades – this is where large families used to live, where the hubbub of children's voices resounded and neighbors shouted the latest news to each other from between the clotheslines.

In 1800, the Jewish community of Lviv numbered around 16,000 people. By 1900, the number had grown to 55,000, a quarter of the city's population at that time. Seventy percent of all doctors, bankers and lawyers were Jewish. Thirty-three percent of university students were of Jewish descent. When the Age of Enlightenment arrived in the community, education became extremely important. The Jewish teachers ranked as the best among their peers. Moreover, there was an equally broad Jewish middle stratum of entrepreneurs: hatters, tailors, hairdressers and also small traders, pawnbrokers and middlemen. There was a limited upper class of wealthy merchants, bankers and leaseholders. The poor class consisted of craftsmen, vendors, chauffeurs, porters, maids and beggars.

Since the nineteenth century, the image of the Jewish community has become more and more colorful, as they made important social, cultural and economic contributions to the city. Many schools, theaters and hospitals were founded. Jewish doctors stood in high regard – not only because of excellent practices and treatment, but also because of their academic research. Yiddish literature was born. The community started to produce engineers and architects. Famous architects designed and built an abundance of buildings just outside of the city center. These buildings, frequently commissioned by a Jewish client or with a Jewish "designation," are among the most beautiful on their street.

On the threshold of World War II one-third of the population belonged to the Jewish community. In former Poland, Lwów was, together with Warsaw and Łódz, the city containing the largest number of Jews. That fact alone makes the destruction of the Jewish culture so dramatic and the search for it so painful.

Between both world wars, Polish politics became increasingly anti-Semitic, in the end even resulting in discriminatory measures against the Jewish population. This and the circumstances of the Jews in Lwów during the first Soviet occupation from 1939 to 1941 will be covered more elaborately in Chapter 4.

Witnesses and backgrounds

There is no better way to understand Lviv than through hearing the stories of the people who experienced it themselves. During our search, we met a number of fascinating eyewitnesses. In each chapter, we concentrate on a meeting that will bring the history to life. Next, we introduce you to the places, buildings, memorials and historical and contemporary background information. We hereby present our three personal witnesses:

Boris Dorfman is the last remaining representative of the Yiddish language and culture in Lviv. He continues to be an ardent supporter of that culture and even teaches Yiddish to a few Ukrainian students. He remembers better than anyone the multicultural atmosphere of prewar Central Europe. What can he tell us about the past, and how does he see the future?

Rabbi Siva Fainerman grew up in prewar Lemberg and is an important representative of the contemporary religious Jewish community in Lviv. He leads a congregation that consists mainly of Russian-speaking members, who came to Lviv from the east after the war. How do they give form to memories and commemoration? How does he proceed while building upon the broken fragments of the past?

Dr. Sharona Igra-Komem is a strong woman who, as a Polish-speaking Jewish girl, witnessed and experienced the pogroms in Lwów. She and her parents survived the Holocaust. Here, she looks back at her youth and at the life that followed. How did she manage to maintain her dignity, and what can we learn from her ill-fated history?

If you walk past the city's storied remnants with this guide in your hand, you will happen upon some splendid buildings that will be difficult to pass by. You will also enter streets into which no tourist will ever set foot and be met with amazed glances. During our explorations, people frequently asked us if we were looking for something when we peered at places that, at first sight, appeared to be uninteresting, such as a garbage dump or a building that was condemned as uninhabitable. However, you will also discover that many districts in and around the immediate town center possess an extraordinary charm – a charm that disappeared in other Central-

European cities a long time ago. It was certainly no coincidence that when Steven Spielberg was looking for a location in which to shoot *Schindler's List*, he ended up in Lviv.

We take you on a journey – either an imaginary one from your living-room armchair or an actual one, a walking tour around this fascinating city. We have tried to introduce you to the "living Jewish Lemberg" from the past and the present. That is no easy task, given the devastation and the limited amount of remaining sources and monuments. Even so, we hope that after walking through "Jewish Lviv," you experience something of the enormous historic significance of the vanished Jewish world of Lemberg.

“Dos Lebn setzt sich fort waiter”

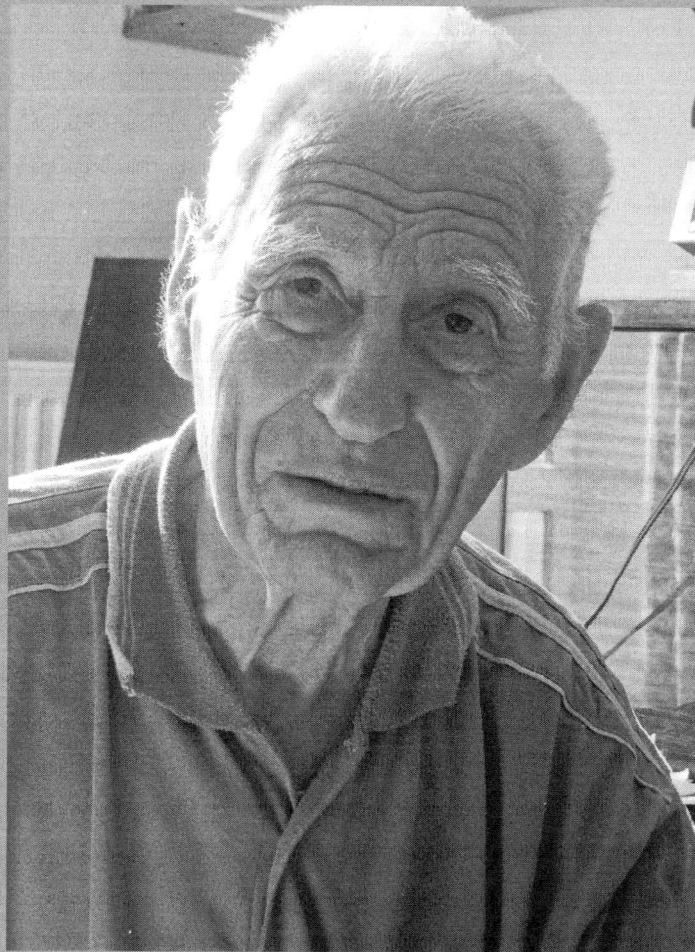

“Dos Lebn set sich fort waiter”

'Life goes on.' An encounter with the very last inhabitant of Lemberik

Shteyt zikh dort in gezele, shtil fartrakht a hayzele
drinen oyfn boydn-shtibl voynt mayn tayer reyzele
yedn ovnt farn hayzl drey ikh mikh arum
kh´gib a fayf un ruf oys: reyzel kum, kum, kum!

(Standing there in the alley, a silent dreamy cottage
Inside in the attic room lives my darling Rejsele
Every evening, I turn around in front of the cottage,
I whistle and call: Rejsel, come, come, come!)

Boris Dorfman. His voice sounds a bit hoarse, as perhaps the voice of an eighty-year-old should sound. Nevertheless, he sings the words clearly and with emphasis. Boris Dorfman has put his glasses on, in order to be able to read the text on the paper. He does his utmost best, knowing that we are listening intently. The language echoes thinly throughout the small room – one that used to resound over the market squares of Lviv, tumbled against the walls of age-old synagogues and connected people with one another in all of Europe... a language that was used to hock wares, negotiate, discuss. The language of the street, the language of a thousand families. Sweet words were whispered in this tongue; many last words as well...Yiddish.

We were lucky to find him at home. After we rang the doorbell two or three times and waited for quite some time, his wife opened the door of the apartment, located a little outside the center of town. Boris is a slight man with a friendly, wrinkled face and gray, bristly hair. He wears shabby clothes and worn sandals. His back is somewhat bent, but never broken by the storms of time. Sometimes, he pats you benevolently on the shoulders, but he is also regularly withdrawn into himself – as often happens with people who have survived all that life can offer. It is Friday afternoon, almost the Sabbath. When the sun goes down, we will have to leave him in peace.

His business card says “journalist.” Boris Dorfman has devoted himself to selling and promoting the limited edition of the Yiddish newspaper *Shofar* wherever it is possible. Because Boris is, above all, an activist, an indefatigable patriot of the Jewish community of Lviv. Sadly, he seems to stand alone.

The couple do not know anybody else in Lviv who still speaks Yiddish. Our conversation is a mixture of Yiddish and German.

Boris Dorfman's life reflects the decline of a language and the tumultuous history of Eastern Europe. He was born on May 23, 1923, in the small shtetl of Gantsjesjty in the Moldovan wine region of Bessarabia. The village is not far from Chisinau (Kishinev), the current capital of the Republic of Moldova – back then a part of Romania. It was a multicultural city. "We all lived together," Boris tells us. "There were Romanians, Germans, Russians, Ukrainians, Greeks, Turks, Bulgarians and a great many Jews."

Boris was brought up with the Yiddish language and Jewish traditions, rules of life and holidays. And yet the family led an active, integrated life. On the maternal side of the family, Russian was spoken. They also knew German and Romanian, the latter being the state language at the time. At home, they read a Romanian and a German newspaper, although their favorite was the Yiddish paper *Unzere Tseyt* (Our Time). He was happy during those first years at school, he recalls. "There were no problems between Christian and Jewish children in my class. We got along very well."

His mother, Molka Dorfman, was an intelligent woman from a family of large landowners; she had received a good education. Furthermore, she was a very active member of the Zionist movement. She anticipated that tensions between the ethnic groups would escalate. An autonomous Jewish state would be a solution for the growing unrest. When Boris was at school, his mother studied Hebrew, Yiddish and Russian; she also followed courses in Jewish history and the Torah. In addition, she administered the fund that collected money to buy land in Israel. Molka's life was imbued with religious occupations – in his memory, Boris sees her praying before him.

At the end of the 1930s more and more Germans arrived in the region. They had fled the west, where the situation for Jews was rapidly deteriorating. Molka organized meetings for them. Alas, in Romania, circumstances also quickly took a turn for the worse. In 1938 the fascists rose to power. Pretty soon thereafter, Jewish schools were forbidden. Boris and his fellow Jewish schoolmates had to sit separately in the classroom. His parents were arrested and incarcerated for a few weeks.

The family placed their hope in the Russians, even though everybody knew about the arrests of millions of people in the Soviet Union and newspapers had reported extensively about the horrors of Stalin's forced-labor camps. "The large majority of the poor Jewish community supported the communist regime," Boris explains. "An eight-hour working day was on the program, laborers would get a better wage and unemployment would disappear. But it worked out differently. The Russians were much worse than we could suspect." In 1940, the Soviet Union annexed Bessarabia in the Molotov–Ribbentrop Pact. The family of Boris's mother was labeled kulak, an independent farmer with his own tract of land. Soviet authorities regarded them as enemies of the people. That meant that all of their land and possessions were taken away from them.

Eventually, Boris's parents were also arrested, accused of anti-Soviet behavior and Zionism. It was a black day. "I remember that day like it was yesterday. I saw everything. The neighbors warned me. If not, I would have been taken away as well. From a distance I saw how they put our belongings – furniture, photographs and jewelry – onto a truck. Only after the war did I see our house again. It was in total ruins."

After the arrest, Boris was allowed to bring food to the prison, but he could not see his parents. His father was soon deported to Kazakhstan. Boris would never see him again; it was not until 1956 that he found out that his father had died in the camp. After a few months, his mother was sentenced – she had to go to a labor camp in the Urals. Boris was allowed to see her one more time, just before she left. "She was confused, but she still had some life in her eyes. We promised to stay in touch."

Boris studied civil engineering. When, in the spring of 1941, the Germans - contrary to the agreements - marched towards the east, the chaos was complete. With great haste, the Russians mobilized their men to survey the borders. Boris and his fellow students were sent to the border as well, tasked with fortifying it. However, the German attack, which began on 22 June, advanced so quickly that not much could be done. For weeks he roamed about, without food, clean water or shelter. By his seventeenth year, he had already experienced what it is to starve. He saw friends die and he himself barely survived.

Boris was a Westerner, as the Russians called the inhabitants of the occupied territories of 1939. They were not sent to the front because the Russians were afraid of treason. So Boris was forcibly employed in Siberia, where he had to build houses for the forced laborers who had come to work in the coal mines; he quickly became a leader. During the war years he continued to correspond with his mother. In 1946, when the Russians had settled the war to their advantage, he returned, destitute and lonely, to Chisinau with his sole possession – a blanket. He managed to conceal the fact that his parents were "enemies of the people." That was his only chance at being allowed to finish the final year of his studies.

There was no lack of work in those postwar years. Because the city was destroyed, people who worked in engineering and construction were in high demand. Finally, in 1947, his mother was released and she immediately resumed her activities with the Jewish community. They lived together in a small apartment. Old times were revived: writers, historians and Jewish theater actors were once again regular visitors. Boris becomes cheerful when he remembers a big party in honor of the famous playwright Sholem Aleichem.

Unfortunately, this prosperity did not last long. After tasting freedom for two years, Molka was arrested once more. This time she was deported to Siberia; Krasnoyarsk was to be her destination. The situation became precarious for Boris as well. He was forced to work for an organization that requisitioned grain. Together with NKVD (People's Commissariat for Internal Affairs) officers, he traveled through the countryside. It was the time of a major famine and Boris knew that the demands made of the villagers were absurdly high. People withholding grain were arrested without mercy and deported; Boris knew that they would never return.

And so, when his mother's nephew offered to let him come to Lviv, he seized the opportunity. He managed to exchange his apartment in Chisinau for a house in Lviv. It would prove to be a decisive moment in his life. He recalls how happy he was with his new accommodations, equipped with a kitchen and a bathroom. Soon he was prospering. Boris became chief engineer at the residential housing department for the Shevchenko district of the city. At the time, Lviv was a nearly empty, unscathed city, from which most of the population had either fled or been deported, or killed. Many displaced people from the eastern parts of the Soviet Union moved to Lviv and also needed to be accommodated.

One of the thousands of families coming to Lviv was that of Betia Rechister (1927). Boris will always remember the moment that he saw her for the first time. "Her father, whom I met at work, liked me and once invited me to a dinner where Betia was as well. It was love at first sight. I was a handsome young man of twenty-eight years. She was four years younger and studied foreign languages at the university. We clearly had a lot in common: we both loved music, theater, poetry and traveling. We got married in 1952 and have been together for sixty years. Our marriage is good; together, we traveled the world."

Stalin died a year after they were married. Boris remembers that day in March 1953: "We were so very happy that that tyrant had gone and hoped that mother would come home soon." That did not happen until 1957. In the meantime, Boris and Betia had welcomed both a son and a daughter. "Mother lived with us in the apartment and helped to take care of the children, to whom she gave a sound Jewish education. Once again, she organized meetings and discussion evenings for the Jewish community, in spite of the constant fear of being re-arrested." In 1963, after six years of freedom, Molka Dorfman died.

Boris was a civil engineer in Lviv for thirty-five years. The very height of his career was his appointment as head of restoration on the Opera House in the 1960s. It was there that he came into contact with theater directors, actors and musicians. He breathed in culture and music – all the more reason to feel the pain in his heart: he had to acknowledge that there was nothing left of that rich Yiddish theater culture. "All the big Yiddish institutes and theaters were destroyed. That whole culture disappeared and will never come back. The Yiddish language died in the 1940s."

In addition to his career, Boris kept working, full of zeal for the Jewish cause – even though the number of Jews in the city amounted to only a few thousand. They were all "imported" from the east and thus spoke Russian. Boris distributed the only Jewish magazine in the Soviet Union, the *Sovyetishe Heymland* (Soviet Motherland). However, only a few people wanted to read it. The number of Jews visibly diminished when they were allowed to emigrate at the end of the 1960s. Many promptly took advantage of the opportunity to escape from the Soviet Union. "Suddenly, they were reminded of their Jewish roots, whereas a lot of these emigrants previously wanted to have little to do with their Jewish identity," Boris says bitterly. His son also left for Israel, where he still lives.

In Lviv, one functional synagogue remained, the New Chassidic Synagogue. However, it was also closed in 1963. When Boris talks about it, he becomes outraged all over again. "The reason was that a hotel was being built nearby, where diplomats and journalists would stay. The Soviet authorities thought that the guests would be disturbed if Jews walked past." The synagogue was transformed into a sports hall.

Since then, the Jews have assembled in private houses. Boris played a pivital role in the small, shattered community, as he knew all the Jews of the city. He distributed Jewish publications and translated books from America and Israel into Russian. During Passover, he distributed matzos to people who were afraid that neighbors would report them when they were preparing this traditional bread.

Boris has been retired since 1986. Now he spends all his time supporting the small Jewish community. His wife Betia is also still active, teaching Hebrew to children and acting as headmistress of the Jewish Sunday school in the New Chassidic Synagogue, which was repossessed by the community after the declaration of independence in 1991. "Students mostly come from mixed marriages. We teach them Hebrew, Jewish traditions, holidays, Jewish songs and dances. The position of the community remains marginal, but at least we can manifest ourselves again. More and more interest in the Jewish past of Lviv is being shown abroad. Sometimes I guide foreign tourists through the city. We have been invited by Jewish organizations in Great Britain, the Netherlands and Germany. And, just as before, I can get by in my language, Yiddish – as long as I meet someone who speaks it."

Boris Dorfman reveals that life in Lviv continues to be difficult. "I am concerned about the nationalism in the city. Economically, these are bad times. The young people are out of work and have no hope. Anti-Semitism is increasing all over Europe, and here as well. The Jews in the city can hardly be bothered with the Jewish traditions – and they do not know any Yiddish. The worst thing is that they call me a "Jewish nationalist," exactly the term the fascists and communists used for me and my mother."

Boris still frequently visits his mother Molka's grave and says his prayers there. Together with Betia, he meticulously observes the Jewish rules and celebrates the holy days. During Yom Kippur, they spend the whole day in the synagogue. Boris cannot act otherwise; this is who he is, even though he is one of the very last. When we ask him how it feels to be the last Yiddish-speaking inhabitant of Lviv, Boris does not really reply.

"Dos Lebn setzt sich fort waiter," is all he says. Then he repeats it: "Dos Lebn setzt sich fort waiter."

It is time. Boris and Betia get ready to go to the synagogue. It is a tiny synagogue on Fedorova Street, where the entrance of the world-famous Golden Rose Synagogue was once situated. We say our goodbyes.

Places of Yiddish culture

Boris Dorfman's life story teems with the strength of Yiddish culture and Jewish religious life. It was imprinted upon his mind from a young age – especially by his mother. Educated as a civil engineer, he found his destiny in the opera and theater world of Lemberg. He became a savior of the nearly eradicated culture by writing for Jewish newspapers and teaching in the Yiddish language.

What traces of that rich Yiddish culture can we find in modern Lviv? Which places can help illustrate Boris Dorfman's life story? How did the Yiddish language thrive among the inhabitants of multicultural Lemberg? Where is the synagogue that survived the war undamaged, but was then used as a sports hall by the communists? And what is the story behind the synagogue where Boris and Betia Dorfman now say their prayers?

The Opera

The Opera House **(1)** features heavily in Dorfman's story. This monumental building dominates the centrally located Prospekt Svobody. From far away, on a beautiful summer's day, one can perceive its radiant white facade through the greenery of the trees along the boulevard. The Opera was built between 1897 and 1900, around the same time as the train station and the university. This was the Golden Age of Habsburg. The city must have looked like one large construction pit during those years. In order to build the Opera House, the Poltva River was diverted underground. Since then, there are no longer any rivers flowing through Lviv.

The Opera House on Svobody Prospekt

The colossal building was constructed in the Viennese neo-Renaissance style. Zygmunt Gorgolewski (1845-1903) was the architect. Many fine artists of the day contributed to the decoration of both the exterior and interior, such as the visual artists E. Pliszewski and P. Wijtowicz and the painters S. Dembicki and M. Harasymowicz. Every inhabitant of Lviv must have been present for at least one performance of opera or ballet, if only to enjoy the elegant fin-de-siècle interior of the great central hall and the foyers.

The Opera House

A ticket costs little and there is a performance almost every night. There is no specific dress code for a visit to the opera. Performances usually begin at around six o'clock in the evening, which means that many Ukrainians go there right after work. Since 2000, the official name of the opera building has been the Lviv National Academic Opera and Ballet Theater named after Solomiya Krushelnytska, the famous Ukrainian soprano who lived from 1872 to 1952. A bust of her stands in the Mirror Hall, a favorite spot for photo shoots.

Solomiya Krushelnytska (1872-1952)

The restaurant on the highest floor of the Magnus department store provides the most beautiful view of the Opera House, with its elegant, decorative angel figures on the roof, and also of the lively streets around it that are usually crowded with cars and pedestrians. **(2)** Magnus was built in 1913, commissioned by the Jewish businessman Frenkel. The elevated position of the rich merchants is evinced by the fact that they were able to erect such a – for that time –modern department store. On the fifth floor, you can see a large photograph of the department store as it appeared before World War II.

A lot of Jewish artists have sung, danced and played in the Opera Theater, but it was not specifically the place for Yiddish theater. However, Joseph Roth penned an article about the "Street of the Legions" (today the Prospekt Svobody) in the *Frankfurter Zeitung* in 1924:

"The high street was once called 'Karl-Ludwig-Straße', out of loyalty to the dynasty. Today it is called die 'Straße der Legionen'. This refers to the Polish legions. It was down this street that Austrian officers once paraded. At present Polish officers walk there. You always used to hear German, Polish, Ruthenian. Now they speak Polish, German and Ruthenian. Around the theater, which demarcates the street at the lower end, the people speak Yiddish. They have always talked that way in this neighborhood. They will probably never talk any differently."

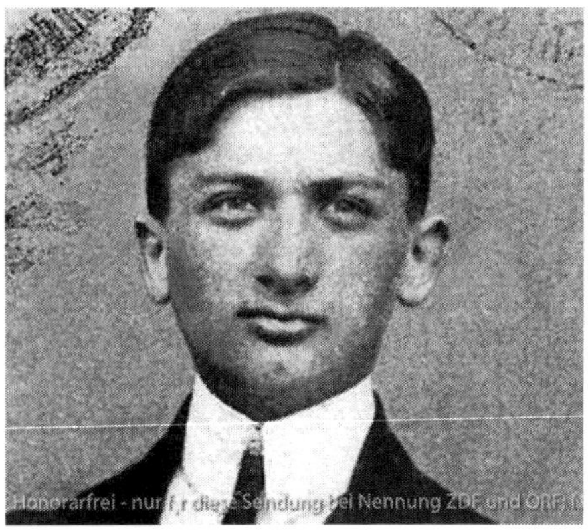

Joseph Roth (1894-1939)

The Yiddish language

For centuries, Yiddish was the language of the street, the market, the shtetl, the songs, the parties, the arguments, the gossip, the love in Central and Eastern Europe. It was a mixed language. It is a fusion of a foundation of German, with elements of Hebrew, Aramaic, Slavic and Romanic languages. It was the daily language in Jewish Lemberik as well. Boris Dorfman uses this name consistently. Yiddish was spoken then, but not written. For most

Jews it was the mother tongue, but at school German or Polish was taught, depending upon who was in power.

If you wanted to keep up with society, those were the languages with which to do so. Whoever wanted to be "civilized" did not speak Yiddish in public anymore. The language symbolized poverty, underdevelopment and the isolation of the ghetto. The liberal Jews of the Haskalah movement (see chapter 3) were a dominant factor in Lemberg in the nineteenth century and held Hebrew in high regard as a study language, but detested the popular Yiddish. They believed that cultured citizens should speak German. Many members of the Jewish intelligentsia, however, also adopted Polish as their language. This situation changed, however, in the beginning of the twentieth century. Young intellectual Jews went searching for their own national identity. They became enthusiastic about Palestine, founded Zionist societies and began to regard the Jewish language in a different light.

Debora Vogel (1902-1942)

A large Jewish language conference took place in the city of Chernivtsi in 1908, during which the participants decided that Yiddish – in addition to Modern Hebrew – must be the national language of the Jewish people. This inspired young writers and poets in Lemberg to write in Yiddish. They sought a connection with modern European literature through an experimental style of writing. Yiddish needed to leave the shtetl and take the high culture by storm.

Lemberg became an important center of Yiddish culture: explosive, creative and with connections all over the world. Important writers from that time are Sholem Aleichem, Sholem Asch and Yitskhok Leybush Peretz. Women were also part of the Yiddish cultural movement, including Debora Vogel (Dvoyre Fogel), Rokhl Korn and Rachel Auerbach. Auerbach wrote about the art of Marc Chagall. Dvoyre Fogel wrote poetry and essays and was friends with the painter Henryk Streng (pseudonym of Marek Włodarski) and the writer-painter Bruno Schulz. Henryk Streng found Fogel dead at her house in the ghetto of Lwów in August 1942, after the massive August Action raid. She had been shot by the Nazis, together with her five-year-old son, Anshel, and her husband.

Three poetesses from Yiddish literature: Kadya Molodowsky, Ida Maze and Rokhl Korn

Sholem Aleichem

One of the most famous literary names that lingers throughout Lviv is that of the writer Sholem Aleichem (Yiddish for "peace be with you"; 1859-1917). Sholem Aleichem's real name was Sholem Rabinovich. He came from a merchant family in the city of Pereiaslav, south of Kyiv. He became world-famous as a result of his work *Tevye the Milkman*, also known as the musical Fiddler on the Roof (Anatevka).

Aleichem is regarded as the writer who aided Yiddish literature in reaching maturity. The daily lives of poor Jewish families in Galicia at the turn of the century are brought to life with much humor and melancholy.

Sholem Aleichem

The great poverty and the threat of pogroms drove many Jews away from Galicia to America, the Promised Land. Sholem Aleichem emigrated to the United States, as did the rest of his family, and for some time he had to wait for his visa in Lemberg. In 1906, he lived on Kotlyarska Street as an emigrant on his way to America. A memorial stone has been placed upon the house in his honor. **(3)**

There is also a Sholem Aleichem Street in Lviv, a side street of Horodotska Street. This street was the cultural center of the Jewish community until World War II. The Union of Jewish Artisans, Jad Charusim, was situated here, but the Jewish Museum was also located here until 1941. **(4)** The artifacts from the museum, which have been salvaged, were housed in various other museums in Lviv, such as the Museum of Ethnography and Art Crafts **(5)** and the Lviv Museum of History of Religion. **(6)** One of the interesting things to see here is a big matzo press. The building on Sholem Aleichem Street currently houses the Alexander Schwarz International Holocaust Center. Alexander Schwarz was born in 1921 in Boryslav and survived the notorious Janowska camp. His father was shot before his eyes; he himself managed to climb out of an execution pit and escaped. He now lives in Munich and dedicates himself, through his foundation, to erecting Jewish memorials in Lviv. A memorial was finally raised in 2003 that commemorates the victims of the Janowska camp, thanks to the Alexander Schwarz International Holocaust Center (see chapter 4).

Plaque commemorating Sholem Aleichem, in the street that is named after him

Finally, there is the Sholem Aleichem Jewish Culture Society, which is committed to reviving Jewish life in Lviv. The society is housed within the Jakob Glanzer Synagogue – which Boris Dorfman calls the New Chassidic Synagogue – in Vuhilna Street. **(7)** More information about the Sholem Aleichem Jewish Culture Society and the Jakob Glanzer Synagogue can be found at the end of this chapter.

Theater

Fascinating Yiddish stage productions were performed in the Jewish Colosseum Theater and in the New Jewish Theater on Hnatyuka Street. The Colosseum was located in the former shopping arcade of a rich Jewish family with the last name of German. The arcade was situated on a distinguished street that led to the theater – this street does not have a name, but it is possible to find the entrance from the Kulisha Street. **(8)** The faded glory of the old grandeur is still visible, although peeling. There are no shops left on the street, but there is a medical station, a beauty parlor and a cafe. At the end is the former Colosseum Theater, three stories high, with a gate to pass through. It is difficult to imagine the former function of the building.

Entrance gate to the former Colosseum Theater

Until the German invasion in 1941, there were no less than sixteen Jewish theater groups in Lwów. Companies from other cities in Poland also performed in Lwów. The repertoire of Yiddish plays was rich and diverse. Sometimes, radio recordings were made of the theater performances.

The New Jewish Theater on the Hnatyuka Street **(9)** was famous as well. It was founded by Yaakov Ber Gimpel in 1889 and was, therefore, called the Gimpel Theater. The theater had to close in 1941, but the building itself is still there and currently houses the First Ukrainian Theater for Children and Youth. It can be a very lively place on certain days, with perhaps the same atmosphere that it had back then: people walking in and out to buy tickets and look at the posters advertising new performances.

Yiddish theater company

Since the 1980s Jewish theater festivals have again been regularly organized in Lviv. Cultural associations are the driving force behind this movement, such as the Hesed-Arieh Fund. During such festivals, plays are performed in the theater on the Hnatyuka Street. However, the language is no longer Yiddish, but generally Russian. As Boris Dorfman says with a sigh, almost nobody still knows Yiddish.

In the spring of 2011, we were deeply moved by the premiere of the play *Janka*, based on the autobiographical book by Janina (Janka) Hescheles. It portrayed a raw version of the Holocaust in Lwów (although the reality was a thousand times worse), as Janka Hescheles had experienced it as a young girl – and survived. The audience was mostly comprised of Jewish inhabitants of Lviv. There was much sighing and crying. The author – a small, delicate lady – was also present and was greatly touched to receive the applause afterwards. The play was written and performed in the Polish language, this was the main language in Lwów in those years.

Shop signs, newspapers and publishers

Which other places of the former Yiddish culture can you see? The signs on shop fronts are the most striking substantiation, as they affirm that Yiddish had occupied a rightful place, next to Polish and German. Some of those signs are still original, such as the ones in Tyktora Street and in Kotlyarska Street. In some other places, such as in Kulisha Street, there are contemporary shop signs with a penchant for nostalgia. **(10)**

Old shop signs in the former Jewish quarter

As chroniclers of Yiddish culture, we should certainly also mention the newspapers, as well as the publishing houses from which they originated. The papers had beautiful names, such as *Der Morgn* (The Morning), *Lemberger Togblat* (Lemberg Daily Paper) and *Neier Morgen* (New Morning). Yiddish could be written in both Hebrew and Latin script. Not all Jewish papers appeared in Yiddish; *Wschód* (East) was a Polish-language Jewish newspaper. **(11)**

Doroshenka Street, at present a lively thoroughfare where streetcars, little buses and many pedestrians press through, was a major center of high-quality economic activity and provision of services. This is evident in the representative fronts of the buildings that were being built here during the large development wave of around 1900. In particular, many Jewish lawyers established themselves in this centrally located street. There were printing offices, such as Jaeger at number thirty-three – you can still see the advertising signs atop the wall on the roof. The publishing house of the Jewish Goldman brothers (1909) was behind the magnificent facade at number nineteen.

Jewish citizens between Yiddish and Polish

Milo Anstadt

Samuel Marek (Milo) Anstadt was born in Lwów in 1920 and emigrated with his parents to the Netherlands as a ten-year-old boy. In Amsterdam, he survived the war by going into hiding and later became a journalist, writer, director and producer. He wrote an impressive autobiography about his childhood years in Lwów, which appeared under the title *Kruis of Munt: Autobiografie 1920-1945* (Heads or Tails: Autobiography 1920-1945). He died on July 16, 2011.

A passage in Milo's book conveys exactly how the Jews in prewar Lwów were caught in the dilemma between identity and assimilation: his grandfather's side of the family felt at home with the Yiddish language, but his mother showed him that the Polish way of life ultimately had more to offer.

"Aside from what was part of life's usual struggles, my grandfather and his family lived in the past. For them, religion was crucial [...] The future related only to the promise of the coming of the Messiah. They lived, in fact, in timeless anticipation and social upheavals that occurred around them barely touched them."

"They felt no connection to the land in which they lived and thought it even unnecessary to learn to speak the Polish language – some babbling was enough for their purposes. They lived in Lwów, but their heart was in Jerusalem, the dream city of two thousand years ago. However, they were not Zionists either, because they did not care for such a modern endeavor. They were not adverse to it, but rather pitying. After all, neither the Torah nor the Talmud proclaimed that the termination of the Diaspora would result from the actions of men."

"My mother's life was oriented towards the future – connected with Jewish traditions, though, but only as long as that yielded no obstacle to her belonging entirely to the world of her time. She was Jewish with the Jews, Austrian with the Austrians, Polish with the Poles. She not only had the capacity, but also the desire to assimilate [...] she wanted to raise her children to be respected citizens. She wanted to get ahead in the world, to amount to something, to radiate the glow of culture. This could not be achieved in the ghetto, but rather outside, in the civil society. Moreover, she was convinced that assimilation was the only remedy against anti-Semitism and she wanted to protect her children by giving them an unassailable Polish facade."

The Chassidic Jakob Glanzer Shul

There were about forty-five synagogues and houses of prayer in Lviv before the war. Afterward, only two remained; all the others had been annihilated by the Germans. In Vuhilna Street, in the small district behind the big market square north of the Opera, you can see one of the remaining synagogues – the Chassidic Jakob Glanzer Synagogue and its associated school. It is a large, square, pale-pink building with high windows, reflecting a vaguely classical style. The building is obviously in a dilapidated state. Before the war, this was the second largest house of prayer in Lwów, after the Great Suburban Synagogue. This house of prayer was built in 1842 and was saved as if by a miracle – maybe because the exterior of the square building does not really resemble a synagogue, perhaps also because the building had such practical dimensions.

The Germans had used it to stable horses and store coaches, which is why there is an interruption in the window placement on the north-facing wall. You can clearly see that an opening was made to create a passageway for the carriages.

Next to the entrance hangs a sign that reads: "The Lviv Sholem Aleichem Jewish Culture Society is housed here." The building gives the impression of being vacant. That impression also applies to the great hall, where the Chassidic congregation once gathered in prayer – if you stand in front of the door, this is on your right. The shul cannot be used as a house of prayer, because the building is in such disrepair. There is an urgent need for maintenance, but there is also a lack of financial resources with which to do so. Some small rooms are used, though, for the activities of the cultural society, as a library and for Betia Dorfman's Sunday school.

Jacob Glanzer Shul

During the daytime, it is mainly elderly men and women walking in and out. If you ask them kindly if you can have a look in the hallway, they will not refuse. If they do not speak any English or German, they will tug on the sleeve of someone who can. Some people enjoy brushing up on their foreign languages and will happily tell you all about themselves.

In the hallway, information panels hang on the peeling walls amid black-and-white photographs, depicting the history of the Holocaust in Lviv, among other things. It is their own place of remembrance although most of these elderly men and women were not born in Lviv or Galicia, but originated from more eastern or southern areas, as did Boris Dorfman. None of them came out of the war undamaged. They pass by these photos every day and have a chat about this and that. The Sholem Aleichem Society is a place where they may find company and conviviality, and if necessary, perhaps sometimes a bit of material support as well.

Entrance to the Lesya Ukrainka Library, where the Jewish Council was located during the German occupation

The building has two floors. The women had their own prayer room on the upper floor, separate from the men. Before the war, you could see beautiful ornaments with Stars of David on the outside of the building. If you walk a little bit closer, towards the busy Prospekt Chornovola, you can still see the remains of the kosher slaughterhouse at your left, behind the fence. Along the Chornovola was a mikvah (ritual bath house).

For a long time after the war, this was the only synagogue where worship services could be held. That lasted until 1963, when the hotel that Boris Dorfman mentioned was built, where Soviet authorities wanted to keep religious Jewish people out of foreigners' sight. The shul was closed. The hall was put to use as a gym. During the years of the collapse of communism, around 1989, the Sholem Aleichem Society took over the upkeep of the building. Thus far, there has been a lack of money with which to restore it. Nearby, just around the corner at 2A Muliars'ka, you will find the building where a Jewish homeless center used to be. For a short while during the war, this building served as the seat of the Judenrat (Jewish Council; see chapter 4). At the moment, a literature museum is established there, named after the Ukrainian poetess Lesya Ukrainka (1871-1913).

Chassidism

Chassidism was and is one of the religious movements within the Judaism of Lviv and Galicia. Furthermore, there are Orthodox Judaism and Liberal Reform Judaism, also called the Haskalah movement. We will go into these movements and the places in Lviv that are connected with them in chapter 3. Boris and Betia Dorfman belong to the New Chassidic community of Lviv.

The Chassidic movement arose in the eighteenth and nineteenth centuries around the so-called "miracle rabbis." They were charismatic rebbes who contributed a mystical experience that was close to everyday life. Their devoutness went hand-in-hand with elated cheerfulness around the Torah. People went to their rebbe for advice about all kinds of daily problems, and also hoped that he could cure their illnesses and ailments with a miracle. Wonderful and humorous stories about the miracles and wise sayings of the rebbes arose during this time.

The rebbes formed dynasties in which the son succeeded the father. Famous centers of Chassidic Judaism in Ukraine are Belz **(12)**, a small town north of Lviv that is worth visiting, and Uman, east of Vinnytsia. To this day, the tombs of the rebbes there are pilgrimage sites for Chassidic believers from Jerusalem and New York.

Rebbe Nachman of Breslov (1772-1810) is worshiped in Uman, and Rebbe Sholom Rokeach (1799-1855; also called Sar Shalom or "Angel of Peace") in Belz, as are his offspring who also occupied the function of rebbe. By some miracle, the dynasty survived the war and was continued in Jerusalem. Friedrich Weinreb (1910-1988), born in Lemberg and raised in the Netherlands, was a Chassidic scholar who enjoyed international fame in the field of Jewish mysticism and interpretation of the Bible. He is very controversial in the Netherlands because of his dubious role during the German occupation.

The Chassidic movement is, moreover, known for its highly traditional beliefs and practices, such as the attire of its members. The black Polish caf-

Current interior of the Jacob Glanzer Shul

Friedrich Weinreb

Martin Buber

tans and large fur hats may be seen in Antwerp, New York and Jerusalem, but you will no longer find them in Lviv. In short, there is a great diversity within the Chassidic movement.

Boris and Betia Dorfman now frequent the prayer services in an annex of what used to be the famous Golden Rose Synagogue, which was destroyed in 1942 (see chapter 3). This annex was also the original entrance to the Golden Rose. Visitors are able to view a cast-iron entrance gate that still contains the screw holes where the Star of David used to be fastened. **(13)** This is where Rabbi Meylakh Sheykhet, who grew up in Lemberg, undertook his fight for the future of the Golden Rose. For him, due to his upbringing in the tradition of Galician Judaism, the Golden Rose is a sacred place. A small group of people faithfully gather here on the Sabbath and on Jewish holidays.

A famous Chassidic inhabitant of Lviv was the philosopher and historian Martin Buber (1878-1965), who was born in Vienna. At the age of six and after his parents divorced, he went to live with his grandparents in Lemberg. His grandfather was the Midrash scholar Solomon Buber (1827-1906), a celebrity in the field of the Chassidic traditions of Eastern Europe. Martin Buber visited the Polish language Franz Joseph gymnasium in Stephan Batoriya Street. The present name of this street is Kniazia Romana Street. The prestigious building now belongs to the Lviv Polytechnic National University. **(14)** After Martin Buber had finished his studies at the gymnasium in Lemberg, he left for Vienna, Leipzig, Zürich and Berlin to continue studying. Following in his grandfather's footsteps, he began collecting Chassidic narratives.

We finish with Milo Anstadt, who shows us that the Chassidim did not always create a merry atmosphere around them. By an early age, this had already completely spoiled his appetite for religion.

"At an early age, I understood that the Jewish lessons, given to me at home every day by a Chassidic teacher of religion, were a concession to my grandfather. My mother thought it an unnecessary burden on a young child; my parents would have preferred that I follow an ordinary course in Modern Hebrew. However, so as not to saddle themselves with the reproaches of my grandfather, when I was six they called in a robust Chassid with caftan and boots, a flaming-red beard and payot (sidelocks). He had to impart piety within me. The rebbe, as we called him, barely spoke Polish and our communication was stiff and awkward."

Yanivske cemetery

One detail of Boris Dorfman's story has yet to be told. Where is his mother's grave that he visits so often? She is buried in the Jewish section of the vast Yanivske cemetery. **(15)** By 1855, the new Jewish cemetery had already been brought into use when the old Jewish cemetery in the Kraków suburb was full. During the Holocaust, both cemeteries were destroyed – the tombstones were used to pave the road to the Janowska camp. Just behind the east entrance, you will find a small column in commemoration of Lviv's victims of the Holocaust. Behind it, the postwar Jewish inhabitants lie buried. Some of the graves have Hebrew texts and a Star of David; another area is in a Soviet style with Russian inscriptions and a picture of the deceased.

Notes

(1) Solomiya Krushelnytska Lviv State Academic Opera and Ballet Theatre (name in English) Address: 28 Prospekt Svobody. Ticket Sales: The ticket office at the entrance of the Opera House Telephone: +380 (322) 72-88-60 Websites: www.opera.lviv.ua

(2) On the corner of Horodotska Street and Szpitalna Street.

(3) 1 Kotlyarska Street.

(4) 11 Sholem Aleichem Street.

(5) 15 Prospekt Svobody.

(6) 1 Muzeina Square (next to the Dominican cathedral).

(7) 3 Vuhilna Street.

(8) The entrance is located between 23 and 25 Kulisha Street.

(9) The former New Jewish Theatre, now the First Ukrainian Theatre for Children and Youth. Address: 11 Hnatyuka Street (It is not directly on the street, but rather set back a little bit, in a courtyard and accessible through a gate.)

(10) Addresses: 1 Tyktora Street, a side-street of Prospekt Svobody, and the little coffeehouse at 8 Kotlyarska Street.

(11) Yiddish Newspapers: The editorial office of the *Neier Morgen* has been housed at 33 Horodotska Street. At 10 Kopernika Street, the former editorial office of the *Lemberger Togblatt* can be found. The Polish-Jewish newspaper *Wschód* was on the corner of 37 Doroshenka Street and Slovatskoho Street. On the ground floor, Zigmund Menashes had a pub called "Maxim."

(12) At www.wikipedia.org, you can find an extensive article about Belz. Furthermore, a few interesting sources: A comprehensive photo gallery from Jola Dziubinska, plus the Belz Memorial Book, can easily be found via www.google.com.

(13) 27 Fedorova Street.

(14) The former Franz Joseph gymnasium is the building on 5 Kniazia Romana Street.

(15) The Yanivske cemetery on Shevchenka Street (Streetcar line 7), although to reach the Jewish section it is better to use the entrance at Yeroshenka Street, east of the cemetery.

L’Chaim!

3. L'Chaim!

'To life!' An encounter with the rabbi of Lviv

"We cannot change the past. We can only change the 'today,' so the future can get better."

A parachutist lands in a tree after a jump. He is completely tangled up in the ropes and his parachute; he cannot possibly free himself. Fortunately, a man passes by. The unlucky fellow manages to stop the passer-by and asks him where exactly it is that he has landed. The man explains in great detail where he is and at the end of his account, he declares that the parachutist obviously has a problem – he is, after all, stuck in a tree with his parachute. To this, the parachutist responds, "You must be a rabbi." "How did you know?" asks the rabbi. "Because you talk a lot and can explain everything, but you will not raise a finger to help me."

Zygmunt Gorgolewski

A conversation with Rabbi Siva Fainerman is like an immersion in stories. He answers every question with an anecdote, narration or legend. Because he is just under fifteen minutes late for our appointment – in Ukraine you may often consider yourself lucky if an appointment goes through at all – he uses this story as an apology. After all, a rabbi is of little use, he wants to say, whereby we conclude that self-mockery is badly needed to survive as a Jewish rabbi in present-day Lviv.

Siva Fainerman breaks the bread, salts it and passes it around, then says a blessing. The rabbi is a wise man who seems to be able to rise above day-to-day worries. His face is lined with little wrinkles; he wears a yarmulke (skullcap) and has a thin gray beard. Olga Shyrokova, one of the most active members of the Jewish community, sits next to him. She translates the rabbi's Russian into broken German.

Most of the Jews in contemporary Ukraine speak Russian. They hail from the eastern parts of the country, or from Russia, and have been looking to the west for a better future. Rabbi Fainerman's work area includes all of Western Ukraine, with the most important synagogues in the cities of Lviv and Lutsk. It is a congregation of about a hundred members and is part of

Reform Judaism. What we would particularly like to hear from him is what it is like to lead a Jewish congregation nowadays. However, we are often sidetracked by history.

The rabbi's life story mirrors part of the history of the Jews in this region. Fainerman was born in Lutsk, a city north of Lviv. Siva means "silver" – his name refers to the fact that his father's hair was already silvery-gray when Siva was born. It was a miracle that the family tree was able to continue. Three months after his birth, in June of 1941, the war reached the city. He and his parents survived the mass slaughter, unlike the rest of the family.

When the war broke out, Siva's mother and her baby were evacuated to Central Asia. She was a nurse and found a job in a mobile clinic on a train, on the front lines. She felt that this was the best way to take care of her child, to create a future for her offspring. Young Siva spent the first years of his life among wounded victims of the front lines.

After the war, mother and son returned to Western Ukraine. They ended up in Lviv, where years later they were reunited with Siva's father. Now that circumstances were more normalized, Siva stayed almost every day in a corner of the sick bay with his mother, who had to work hard to be able to provide for them. Fortunately, the boy was healthy, despite the peculiar circumstances in which he grew up.

There is no doubt that Siva inherited his expressive method of storytelling from his father. Father Fainerman taught his son about Jewish traditions by telling him stories; indeed, to give actual lessons from books was not allowed in the Soviet Union. Siva spoke Yiddish with his father, but when the latter died in 1962, he stopped speaking the language. After all, Siva no longer knows anybody who speaks it.

At school, Siva received the same communist education as all other children. At first, he was very enthusiastic about it. "One day, I came home and resolutely told my mother that I thought that all capitalists should die. She was surprised but reacted calmly. She gave me a knife and said, 'How do you want to do that? Do you really want to fight with millions of people? Start with the chickens in the courtyard.' There I stood helplessly, near the chickens, the knife in my hands."

After the Soviet Union disintegrated, Siva lost his job as an engineer. Due to the stories that his father had told him, the Jewish tradition was precious to him. He began studying to be a Jewish teacher. There were only a few prayer leaders at the time, and so he became a rabbi quite quickly. These days, he is in charge of the liberal synagogues in Lviv, Lutsk and Uzhhorod. Thus, the rabbi travels a lot.

We ask Fainerman what it is like to build up a Jewish synagogue and to lead a congregation in a city where Jews have been so decimated. The rabbi responds to this question every time with only a few short and modest words: "It is not because I am a hero, as I certainly am not." He concludes, "God told me that I had to do it; who am I to say no?"

We also ask the rabbi if he has ever lost his faith, after the terrible things that happened to the Jews. Fainerman also replies to this question with a story: "A man attended the synagogue. But he had to cry so hard that he could not pray. The rabbi asked him why he did not pray. In tears, the man told his life story. A lot of terrible things had happened to him. His wife had died; he had to work hard and take care of his six children all by himself. But fate struck again – his house burned down, so his cow died and even his prayer books were destroyed. 'Why would I still pray to God? And where was He in the Holocaust?' The rabbi answered him: 'These are matters for which you should not reproach God. Man is responsible for the evil. You can ask yourself why this had to happen specifically to you – that might seem unjust. But people are not robots. Man has free will and the duty to choose between good and evil, again and again.'"

The rabbi considers it his duty to concentrate on the future, although he agrees that memorialization occupies an important role in Lviv. "I remember a commemoration near the monument at the former Janowska camp. We said Kaddish to mourn the dead at the wall of the extermination camp. That was very emotional and impressive. A young woman was present at this commemoration; she was a volunteer from South Africa. "She wept loudly and was inconsolable. I held her by the shoulders and said, 'Stand up. Crying does not help. We cannot change the past. We can only change the present, so the future can get better.'"

Anti-Semitism is one of the contemporary problems. Olga Shyrokova has the feeling that it is growing in Ukraine every year. When she was still working in an office, people would regularly call her names because of her Jewish background. "At a certain moment, I got so fed up with it that I had had enough. I withdrew into our own community."

She now teaches Hebrew and Jewish dance and music to the children. One of the few activities she undertakes outside of the community is the tours she gives of "Jewish Lviv."

"For us, the question is always whether we should assimilate or keep ourselves separate from the world. However, isolating oneself is often counterproductive. In the old days, Jews built a wall around their quarter in the medieval center of Lviv. This has not helped. There is a story going around in Lviv about two rabbis: one built a synagogue with a heavy, robust iron roof and the other rabbi, one with ordinary roof tiles. Eventually, the house of prayer with the iron roof was destroyed, while the other one remained upright. In the end, perhaps it is better to succumb a little to the prevailing views, to assimilate and adapt. But that is difficult in a region that has always been scourged by anti-Semitism. However, the choice is ours. It is most important to try to remain as dignified as possible."

Rabbi Siva Fainerman uses firmer words: "Anti-Semites want to amputate one particular community from the population. But they will never succeed – that much has been proven here in Lviv. Those people are deranged, mentally ill. Someone should invent a medicine to treat them." Olga Shyrokova adds, "The citizens of Lviv regard themselves as 'civilized Europeans.' But these are often just words. People still think of us in a very negative way."

We talk about the old sanctuaries of the Jews and what the rabbi thinks of the idea that some of them might be restored. "That, in turn, would create a new job for me," the rabbi jokes. He understands that it is attractive for the city to draw tourists by showing Lviv's Jewish past, but he is critical. "An example is the restaurant 'At the Golden Rose,' established a few years ago next to the ruins of the synagogue that was once so famous. This place is sacred to us. People were murdered there. It is not good when people eat, drink and have fun at this spot." What, then, does he think about the Kraków Market, which has been built on the location of the centuries-old cemetery? "That was the cemetery for people who died of natural causes. It is no less terrible that that place disappeared, but it does make a difference."

Even though only a small percentage of the prewar Jewish population is left in Lviv, the mutual differences have not diminished. Rabbi Siva Fainerman stands in the tradition of Reform Judaism; this allows for a freer interpretation of Halakha. Halakha is the Jewish religious law with Jewish precepts. "Some Orthodox Jews think that a Jewish man should not be buried next to his Christian wife. For instance, I do eat kosher, but I place a freer interpretation on other precepts, such as those regarding burials. I bury the Jewish husband next to his Christian wife, say Kaddish for them and recite both their names at the annual commemoration of the dead."

Finally, we talk about the future. "Since Ukrainian independence, more Jews are coming to Lviv again," says Olga. "They come primarily from Israel, like my neighbors, a family with six children. They thought Israel was too dangerous and did not want their children to grow up there. A few years ago, I traveled through Israel myself. I felt a lot of tension. I prefer living here."

We drink another glass, toasting: "May the different Jewish communities in Ukraine flourish again!" For the photo that we wanted to take, Rabbi Siva Fainerman donned his yarmulke. Then, we drank to life again - l'chaim – although the rabbi kept kosher by drinking water.

Places of Jewish life today

Walking around the northern part of the old center of Lviv and the site of the Kraków Market, you might suddenly stumble across an empty plot. A small patch of grass between the weathered, yellow-ochre houses, usually slightly elevated, perhaps with a little playground and a few benches, surrounded by trees… or an empty place, paved with broken tiles that creates a too-large passageway between residential blocks... or something similar to a plaza but at a strange angle, with an indefinable aura. Chances are, you will eventually arrive at a spot where one of the approximately forty-five synagogues and houses of prayer of Lviv/Lemberik once stood. The Jewish past speaks incisively and inescapably through these blank spaces. What once existed leaves a trace behind – scars in the city. Like pulled teeth in a jaw, Lviv is a wounded city.

That which was built with faith, hope and love over the centuries was wiped from the face of the earth by hatred and rage in a very small amount of time. Almost all of the synagogues and prayer houses of Lviv were destroyed by the Germans in 1941 and 1942. As a follow-up to the stories of Rabbi Siva Fainerman and Olga Shyrokova, we want to tell the story behind these empty places.

The Jewish quarter in the medieval city center

Tourists generally begin their journey in the center of town, at Ploshcha Rynok in Lviv; it is the market square with wonderful facades all around, with the proud town hall in the middle, and Greek gods and goddesses as guardian angels on the corners. Serbska Street begins in the southeast corner of the square; if you enter it, you will quickly cross the Staroyevreiska Street, the Old Jewish Street. This is where we encounter the stories of Rabbi Siva and Olga.

Staroyevreiska Street was the heart of the medieval city center. This street and a few streets around it formed the medieval ghetto, to which Olga referred when she said, "Jews built a wall around their quarter." However, this isolation was not a choice of their own making – it was compulsory for the Jews to live in a ghetto. At first, the quarter was a bit more to the north, outside of the city walls around Staryi Rynok (the Old Market Square).

Later, after a big fire raged there in 1352 and the number of people quickly increased, the Jews were allocated a small plot of land within the old city walls.

That is where the richer Jews went. The ghetto had a massive gate that was closed when darkness fell. That gate, which dated back to the sixteenth century, was situated at the spot where Fedorova Street leads to Ruska Street. Nowadays, the only parts still visible are the broad buttresses that used to flank the gate at both corners.

There was not much space in the Jewish quarter. The families were large; new people poured in from outside of the city and the only solution each time was to build a new floor on top of the houses – that is why the houses here are tall and narrow. If you walk down these streets, have a good look through the gates to discover the picturesque - although usually quite damp - courtyards with their surrounding railings. The streets were the domain of the street vendors and market women. This is where learned men hastened to their synagogues and houses of study (beth hamidrash) at the end of Staroyevreiska Street, next to the old city wall. The women went the same way in order to frequent the ritual bath, the mikvah. On some of the houses, you can still see a narrow, rectangular notch next to the door where the mezuzah used to hang. A mezuzah is a piece of parchment inscribed with Hebrew verses from the Torah, which was placed inside a small case and attached to the doorposts of Jewish houses. You will find traces of such mezuzah sites at various entrances within the quarter. **(1)**

Two synagogues and a restaurant

After walking all the way to the end of Staroyevreiska Street in the direction of the city wall, you will arrive at a deserted area. To the right is the place where the Great City Synagogue, the Synagoga Civilis, **(2)** stood until 1942; it was built between 1795 and 1801. It was the largest house of prayer in Lemberik. Now all that is still visible is its foundation.

At your left side, a corrugated iron fence obstructs the view of the remains of another synagogue that stood here until 1942: the famous Golden Rose **(3)**. This synagogue was considered one of the most beautiful synagogues in all of Europe. Two pointed arches of the northern wall, with bricked-up window recesses, still remain. A memorial stone to the left of the ruins reminds visitors in three languages – Ukrainian, Hebrew and English – that the synagogue, built in 1582, was destroyed by the Nazis in July 1942.

The best way to see what remains is from the terrace of the restaurant-tavern *Pid Zolotoyu Rozoyu* (At the Golden Rose), which was established here in 2008. Perhaps, however, there is an opening in the fence somewhere.

On its website, the tavern promotes itself by saying, "This is perhaps the only tavern in the Ukraine where there are no listed prices. Here, you can actually haggle over your final bill" – which revives the anti-Semitic stereotype of Jews being eager for money.

Whether or not it is tasteful to set up a bar/restaurant in a "Jewish style" next to the destroyed and not-yet-rebuilt synagogue is debatable. Rabbi Fainerman does not have a good word to say about it: "This place is sacred to us. People were murdered there. It is not good when people eat, drink and have fun at this spot." The website also states: 'There is a cosy terrace in perhaps the quietest area of Lviv' – without including any information about the reason for this 'quietness'.

The Golden Rose as it used to be

The fence of the Golden Rose

Past and future of the Golden Rose

The Golden Rose was a private synagogue built in 1582 by the chairman of the Jewish community, Izak Nachmanowicz. The synagogue was constructed on the site of a former brothel and its official name was Turei Zahav Synagogue ("Columns of Gold"); this was the title of an authoritative Halachic commentary on Jewish law that had been written by David HaLevi Segal, a famous rabbi at the synagogue between 1654 and 1667.

However, everyone knew the beloved synagogue by its nickname, Di Goldene Royz, the Golden Rose. There is a legend connected to that name. Twenty years after the synagogue was built, a conflict flared up between the Jewish congregation and the Jesuits. The Jesuits took possession of the building and wanted to build themselves a church on this spot. In 1609, after three years of bitter fighting and subsequently paying a ransom of 20,600 guilders, the Jewish community had the synagogue returned. A legend that was published for the first time in 1863 attributes this restitution to Rosa bat Ya'akov, Izak Nachmanowicz's daughter-in-law. She may have brokered the deal with the Jesuits; some say that she had prostituted herself to placate them, and afterward took her own life. Perhaps this story is part of the anti-Semitic repertoire, as well. In any case, her role was essential and in honor of Rosa bat Ya'akov, the building received the name Golden Rose.

There was a large celebration when the synagogue was returned. Yitzhak ben Shemuel HaLevi, who was rabbi at the time, composed Shir Ge'ula

(Song of Deliverance), which compared the return of the synagogue to the salvation of the Jews from Egyptian and Babylonian captivity.

A synagogue did not serve merely as a house of prayer; it was also a center for Jewish activities. It was simultaneously a cheder (school), library, kosher slaughterhouse and ritual bathhouse. Furthermore, there were rabbis present day and night to give advice and pass judgment in religious disputes. The Golden Rose and the Great City Synagogue had a library **(4)**, ritual bathhouse **(5)** and a hospital **(6)** as well and all were reachable from within the building. The entrance of this complex of buildings was located at the same address as that of the Nachmanowicz family.

The site where the Great City Synagogue once stood

The Center for Jewish Art at the Hebrew University of Jerusalem has been thoroughly investigating the building history of the Golden Rose. There are plans to reconstruct the synagogue, but they are not yet able to reach an agreement regarding the architectural concept; for the time being, it is an open proposition as to how the project will be financed. Developers look enviously at this superior location. At the end of 2011, there was even a plan to build a hotel on the site, in order to accommodate soccer fans who would come and visit the city during the European soccer championship.

Scale model of the old city center – in the circle at the left is the Golden Rose, at the right, the Great City Synagogue

The Lviv city council squabbled for a long time about what to do with the ruins of the Golden Rose. Should it be a center of commemoration for the Jews of Lviv, or should it perhaps become an active synagogue once again? In a house adjacent to the Golden Rose, prayer services are being held by a small group of dedicated Orthodox-Chassidic Jews, led by Rabbi Meylakh Sheykhet. They wish for the Golden Rose to be reinstated as a synagogue. Boris and Betia Dorfman also belong to this group. The work of restoration and conservation of the ruins of the Golden Rose Synagogue began in 2016, commissioned by the Office of Historic Environment Preservation of Lviv City Council. The project includes revaluation of the site of the Golden Rose Synagogue, the Great City Synagogue, as well as marking the site of the Beth Hamidrash. The 'space of synagogues' will be designed as a commemorative space. Rebuilding of the Golden Rose Synagogue is not foreseen in the plan.

Reform Judaism and the Tempel

Rabbi Fainerman is a teacher and prayer leader of the liberal Jewish community of Lviv. Its name, B'nai B'rith, means "Children of the Covenant." This is a small congregation that gathers on the Sabbath and Jewish holidays in the Jewish cultural center on Kotlyarevskoho Street. **(7)**

It is a congregation without a synagogue at the moment, but in the past its house of prayer, the Tempel Synagogue, shone just a stone's throw from the Opera House – the building dominated Staryi Rynok (the Old Market) northeast of the Opera. The site is now a slightly inset square along the busy Khmelnytskoho Street.

The site of the Tempel on Staryi Rynok, with the memorial stone

In the middle sits a small, rather neglected park. A memorial stone reminds people in Ukrainian and English about the synagogue of the Progressive Jews, which had dominated the square for a hundred years and was blown up in August of 1941, shortly after the German invasion. The text fails to mention that this happened when a service was being conducted, so that many succumbed to the fire or were killed by the walls that fell down on them. It was only in the 1990s that the memorial stone was allowed to be erected by a Jewish organization that had raised the money itself. In 2011, greenery was planted around it and the anti-Semitic graffiti of swastikas was removed. The other statue in the park has nothing to do with the former synagogue. It is an abstract sculpture of a lion, the symbol of Lviv.

At the northeast side of Staryi Rynok, you will find Lviv's oldest church, the Church of Saint John the Baptist from the thirteenth century. However, after the Tempel was built, it dominated the market square with its enormous dome and overshadowed the little church. This says a lot about the importance of the Jewish community in nineteenth-century Lemberg. In the church is a permanent exhibition of archaeological finds, old pen-and-ink drawings and scale models of the city in ancient times. On one of the models, you can see how the Golden Rose and the Great City Synagogue must have looked within the walls.

The liberal or Progressive Jewish community was established in Lemberg in the first half of the nineteenth century. "Reform Judaism" is another name for this movement, because they wanted to modernize Jewish traditions and rituals. The Hebrew name for this movement is Haskalah, or Jewish Enlightenment. Its roots lie in eighteenth-century Germany, resulting from the influences of the Enlightenment, modern science and the political commitment to full civil rights for Jews. The Progressive Jews advocated assimilation into modern culture. In 1843, the city of Lemberg granted the liberal Jewish community permission to build a synagogue.

The design of the synagogue should have a modern appeal. The model for the Tempel was to be the Reform synagogue in Vienna, the capital of the Habsburg Empire, to which Lemberg belonged. The floor plan of the Tempel was in the shape of the Star of David. A massive dome crowned the building. The style of this dome perfectly complemented the Baroque Christian church buildings in the city, such as the Dominican Church.

The message was: we maintain our identity, but we keep up with modern times. This implies that the Jews felt at home in Lemberg and that they were a part of the culture of the city. Rabbi Abraham Kohn consecrated the Tempel in September 1846. The local newspaper wrote that it was an impressive ceremony and that German psalms were sung. There was even an organ in the Tempel. On the facade of the Tempel, two texts are written in Hebrew: "O house of Jacob, come, let us walk in the light of the Lord" (Isaiah 2:5) and "This is the gate of the Lord" (Psalm 118:20).

Milo Anstadt treasures special memories of visiting the liberal synagogue of Lemberg as a boy: *"Our next-door neighbor, Zysjoe Blaustein, a high school student of sixteen, sometimes took me with him to the liberal synagogue. Things happened very differently there than in the [Chassidic] shul of Grandfather Keller. For one thing, they never spoke any Yiddish, only Polish and sometimes Modern Hebrew. It was generally the Zionists, who advocated for a Jewish State in Palestine, who attended the liberal synagogue. Also Jewish intellectuals – who had a vague religious relationship with Judaism and who did not regard themselves as Polish-Jewish, but rather Jewish-Polish – frequented it. They were confident that civilization would surely expel anti-Semitism."*

"In the liberal synagogue, which was called Tempel, they played the organ and a men's choir sang. I liked the service more – it was much more cheerful than in Grandfather's shul and I often asked Zysjoe if I could come with him on the summery Friday evenings. And then, if I came home later, my father urged me not to tell Grandfather that I had been to the Tempel. I did not ask why, because I had already known for a while that being a Jew was very different for one person than it was for another." (Milo Anstadt, *Kruis of Munt* (Heads or tails).

However, the radical adjustments to modern times were extremely disagreeable to the Orthodox Jews and the Chassidim. Soon after the inauguration of the Tempel, a violent conflict broke out between the various Jewish groups in Lemberg.

The story of Abraham Kohn

Rabbi Abraham Kohn

Rabbi Abraham Kohn (1807-1848) was the first rabbi of the Progressive community. In 1844, he was appointed Chief Rabbi of the Jewish congregation in Lemberg. He was a highly intellectual man, gentle and driven by the ideal of reforming Judaism. He had received his education at the University of Prague. In Lemberg, Kohn was the driving force behind the construction of the new synagogue and campaigned for better education for Jews in the city. The Progressive Jews had propagated German culture, language and literature – above Polish and Yiddish – and strove towards secular education for Jews. As far as politics was concerned, Kohn proved himself to be a progressive man. In the revolutionary year of 1848, he supported the Polish independence movement in its battle for Galicia's national autonomy.

The conflict between Progressive and Orthodox Jews in Lemberg arose not only because of the new Tempel and its modern worship, but also due to the undercurrent of a political conflict. In the Habsburg Empire, by law, taxes had to be levied on kosher meat and Shabbat candles. In Lemberg, these taxes were collected by a committee of Jewish Orthodox leaders, who also enriched themselves with those taxes. For Rabbi Kohn, the duty to hand over taxes for religious matters went completely against the principles of equal civil rights. He rebelled openly against the humiliating tax, levied only on Jews, and came into conflict with the Orthodox leaders.

It remains unclear if this or his religious urge to reform perturbed the establishment, but the fact remains that Rabbi Abraham Kohn was assassinated in his own home by a fanatical Jewish extremist. On 6 September 1848, a young man sneaked into the Kohn's kitchen and poisoned the soup. Rabbi Kohn and his youngest daughter, Theresa, died the next day. The perpetrator was arrested. The Kohn family's maid was the key witness in the trial. She testified that she had seen a pale, skinny man in a dark coat enter the kitchen, wanting to light his cigar at the fire, who had clearly been messing around near the soup.

It was only after ten years that the Jewish congregation of Lemberg received a new chief rabbi. However, from that day on, there would consistently be two chief rabbis in Lviv: one Progressive, the other Orthodox. **(8)**

Around the Sianska Street, formerly Synagogi Street

We take you now to Sianska Street, a part of the old district behind the Opera House. These streets used to belong, together with Staryi Rynok, to the Kraków suburb. This was a center of Jewish life in Lemberg.

At one time, there were six synagogues and associated buildings very close to each other on and around Sianska Street, which was called Synagogue Street until 1871. At the moment, these streets are located at the back of a lively market or "bazaar"; there are quite a few such bazaars in Lviv and you can find all your daily needs there. Numerous stalls offer a wide variety of clothing, shoes, food and "luxury" goods, and in the middle there is a covered market hall for vegetables, fruit and meat. At the rear, old women do their best to sell some potatoes, cabbage and fruit from their gardens or fresh milk and cheese from their cows. They are often checked by policemen, who chase them away if they do not have a permit. This occasionally results in minor riots.

Where the streetscape was previously defined by synagogues on both sides, it is now a disorganized, open area, with neglected greenery or a playground. To the left and right are broad stone steps leading up to places where, at the moment, nothing noteworthy is left. When you stand at the halfway point on Sianska Street, you can imagine how the district was once arranged.

The Great Suburb Synagogue, built in 1633, stood at the center of the street. **(9)** On the edge of the park with the playground, on the side of an old house, a monument has been placed in memory of this synagogue and also of the Beth Hamidrash Yeshiva (the Torah school) and its library. All of these sanctuaries were decimated in the summer of 1941. The commemorative tablet states in Ukrainian, English and Hebrew: "On this site stood the grand synagogue Out of the Walls, including a study center for the Bible. It was built in the middle of the seventeenth century and was reconstructed in the nineteenth. It was destroyed by the Nazis in August 1941."

The commemorative tablet is regularly defaced with swastikas or with the Star of David hanging from gallows, as are so many other Jewish places in Lviv. These days, the council seems to take more care in keeping the Jewish monuments clean. However, as became apparent from the stories of Rabbi Siva and Olga Shyrakova, anti-Semitism is still present everywhere, lying just beneath the surface of Ukrainian society. A communal effort to learn about the Holocaust and how it could happen – including the dubious role of the Ukrainian nationalists – has hardly begun.

A bit further along, there used to be a synagogue that belonged to the Beth Lechem Society **(10)** and at the end of the street stood the Chassidic Schleyen Synagogue. **(11)** This house of prayer was built in 1897 by architect Arthur Schleyen and was set on fire during the anti-Semitic pogrom of

The Schleyen Synagogue after the destruction

1918, amidst the Polish-Ukrainian civil war. The ruins of the burned building are visible in the only photograph that was preserved.

Only two synagogues endured the war, albeit not unscathed. One is the Jakob Glanzer Shul, discussed in chapter 2. The other one is the Beis Aharon V'Yisrael Synagogue, also known as Tsori Gilod Synagogue, on Brativ Mikhnovskykh Street. **(12)** In this street, which is a bit remote, sits a yellow building that is guarded from unwanted visitors by a high wall. The synagogue was built in 1924, after a design by Albert Kornblut. The interior has magnificent murals on the walls and ceilings (restored in 2004-2005), but, unfortunately, the building is not open for tourist visits. When the Nazis came, they desecrated this house of prayer by turning it into a horse stable. After the war, the Russians used the building as a warehouse. It was not until 1989 that it was finally returned to the Jewish community. Rabbi Mordechai Shlomo Bald and his wife Sarah, who hail from Brooklyn, New York, lead the Orthodox-Chassidic congregation of approximately five hundred members. They also started a cheder, a Jewish school.

The site of the synagogue on Sianska Street, with its commemorative plaque – now a children's playground

The Jewish school of Lviv

The Jewish school "Brativ Izrailyu" (Brothers of Israel) lies in the heart of the Lviv district of Sykhiv. It is a big building with a garden, courtyards and a playground. From the street it is not obvious that there is a school there, but inside the atmosphere is cheerful. In the central hall, children are dancing and singing. Many drawings and Hebrew and Ukrainian texts decorate the walls. The boys wear yarmulkes (skullcaps) or caps, but otherwise the children would not stand out as any different in the street. Only the rabbi's sons wear payots, the traditional long sidelocks.

The principal Sarah Bald welcomes us with tea and cookies. She is the wife of the orthodox rabbi of Lviv. The couple hail from New York, but has been living in Lviv since 1994. It took them twenty years to found the school and make it into what it is today: an elementary school and a Jewish gymnasium. The school now has one hundred and fifty students aged from six to sixteen years, who come from Lviv and the surrounding area.

There is quite a lot of poverty and social problems in the city, therefore the school has a social function as well. The Balds provides food, clothing and sometimes financial help for Jewish families. They also organize exchanges with Jewish schools in Great Britain, Israel and North America.

Sarah and her husband were raised with rich Jewish traditions. They consider it their duty to share that cultural wealth in Lviv. According to Sarah, many Jewish parents struggle with the heritage of the Soviet period. During the period of the Soviet Union traditions were concealed. Even now, parents are reluctant to send their children to the Jewish school, out of fear of discrimination. That is why many Jewish children assimilate with their Ukrainian environment and subsequently their traditions are lost. Sarah explains not only to the children, but also to the parents that they don't need to keep their ceremonies quiet and unobtrusive anymore, such as was necessary in the past. Ukraine is a free country now.

The old Jewish cemetery

The Jewish cemetery on the Kraków Market

Rabbi Siva also mentioned the cemetery on the site of the Kraków Market. What is the story of that cemetery?

Prospekt Vyacheslava Chornovola, an exit road with a lot of busy traffic, borders on the Kraków suburb. At the opposite side, behind Hotel Lviv – a solid building from the Soviet era – begins the region of the Kraków Market. The terrain looks different there. The buildings are higher, the streets more metropolitan. Everything shows that this must have once been a prosperous neighborhood. This is where, since the nineteenth century, the Jewish middle class moved to. Originally, these run-down facades were beautiful, with marvelous bay windows and the occasional richly ornamented wrought-iron balconies; there used to be many shops and businesses here. This is where the social and economic lives of well-to-do Jewish people took place. Suddenly, behind a junction of five streets, there is a lot of commotion – it is the entrance to the Kraków Bazaar. This is the area where the big Jewish cemetery used to be.

The Kraków Market, on the banner above the gate: "Welcome to our market"

The Jews have buried their dead here for a thousand years. Since early on, the cemetery was famous all over Eastern Europe as a tourist attraction. From far and wide, people came here to visit the graves of their ancestors, or just to admire. In 1855, the cemetery was already closed, simply because it was full. At that time, between twenty-five and thirty thousand people were buried there. It is now a large market with hundreds of stalls and small shops for clothing, luxury goods and provisions. It teems with thousands of people who come looking for things to their liking. It is unimaginable that the site of the former Jewish cemetery is right under this lively center – where the population of Lviv is finding itself again after sixty years, building a new existence. Probably, nobody gives much thought to how much guilt this place holds – because, why should they? The people here have just faced a history of their own, from which the horror has been ebbing away for only a few decades.

Nothing of the cemetery remains to be seen, apart from a few sections of the original wall running along Rappaporta and Kleparowska Streets. The Germans made Jewish forced laborers remove the tombstones and then ordered them to build, among other things, an access road to the Janowska concentration camp with these stones. The cemetery was subsequently bulldozed. The Kraków Market confirms – in an almost apocalyptic way – the unbelievable events of this city. Not only did the Nazis kill the Jews themselves, but they even tried to wipe out the dead of Lemberik.

The old Jewish cemetery (besojlem – Hebrew for "house of eternity") was recorded for the first time in the year 1414. In the following centuries, this sacred place was constantly expanded until, in the seventeenth century, it covered the whole area between Rappaporta Street, Bazarna Street, Brovarna Street and Kleparivska Street – approximately three hectares. The two Jewish communities (in the old city and the Kraków suburb) shared the cemetery.

After the war, in 1947, the market was built. The stones that were left were used to build a segment of the wall of the bazaar. Nowadays, the green plot behind the hospital is the only remaining place where you can – although very remotely – still catch a whiff of the atmosphere of the former cemetery. The City Council of Lviv is developing plans to build a monument at this site, as a tribute to the destroyed Jewish cemeteries of Galicia.

The Jewish Hospital

The Jewish hospital

Rabbi Siva Fainerman's mother worked as a nurse during and after the war; the hospital was the setting in which he grew up. This was not the Jewish hospital on Rappaporta Street **(13)**, but we shall use his story as a pretext to tell more about that Jewish hospital.

It is one of the few Jewish buildings whose exterior fared reasonably well during the years of horror – and it is an extremely beautiful building. The finest view of the hospital and its colorful mosaic domes is accessible from Horodotska Street.

The hospital was built in 1899, on the site of another Jewish hospital that had been there for more than a century. Next to it was a "Home for the Elderly," built in 1880. The hospital was constructed in an extraordinary "neo-Moroccan" style. Stars of David were inlaid within both the dome and the facade. The hospital was regarded as very modern for its time, with an annexed kitchen, laundry, mortuary and even a cafeteria. The management of the hospital was influential within the community, administrating most of the Jewish cemeteries, bathhouses and ritual slaughterhouses. It also provided lessons in personal hygiene to students and the poor. According to its records, the majority of the hospital's patients were Jewish, but not all of them. During and after World War I, one-third of the patients were Christian. Today, the hospital functions mostly as a maternity unit: people regularly pass by with presents for newborns. You can even visit the garden of the hospital, a beautiful, quiet place where you can find a moment of peace and tranquility.

Notes

(1) Traces of such mezuzah sites can be found at the entrance to 4 Ruska Street, at 20 and 27 Fedorova Street, 48 Staroyevreiska Street and 21 Brativ Rohatyntsiv Street.

(2) Place: Staroyevreiska Street, next to the house at number 50.

(3) The ruins of the northern wall can be seen from Staroyevreiska Street, from the terrace of the restaurant *Pid Zolotoyu Rozoyu* (At the Golden Rose). The official entrance of the Golden Rose Synagogue was at 27 Fedorova Street, but is no longer accessible.

(4) 41 Staroyevreiska Street.

(5) 7 Arsenalska Street.

(6) 29 Fedorova Street.

(7) 30 Kotlyarevskoho Street.

(8) Michael Stanislawski has written a fascinating book about the struggles of Rabbi Kohn in Lemberg and the trial after the murder: *A Murder in Lemberg: Politics, Religion, and Violence in Modern Jewish History* (Princeton: Princeton University Press, 2007).

(9) Sianska Street, where the park with the playground is currently located.

(10) Between Sianska Street and Mstyslava Udatnoho Street (north of Sianska Street).

(11) On the corner of Sianska and Lasneva Streets.

(12) 4 Brativ Mikhnovskykh Street.

(13) Rappaporta Street, at the T-junction with Leontovycha Street.

‘See you next year in Jerusalem’

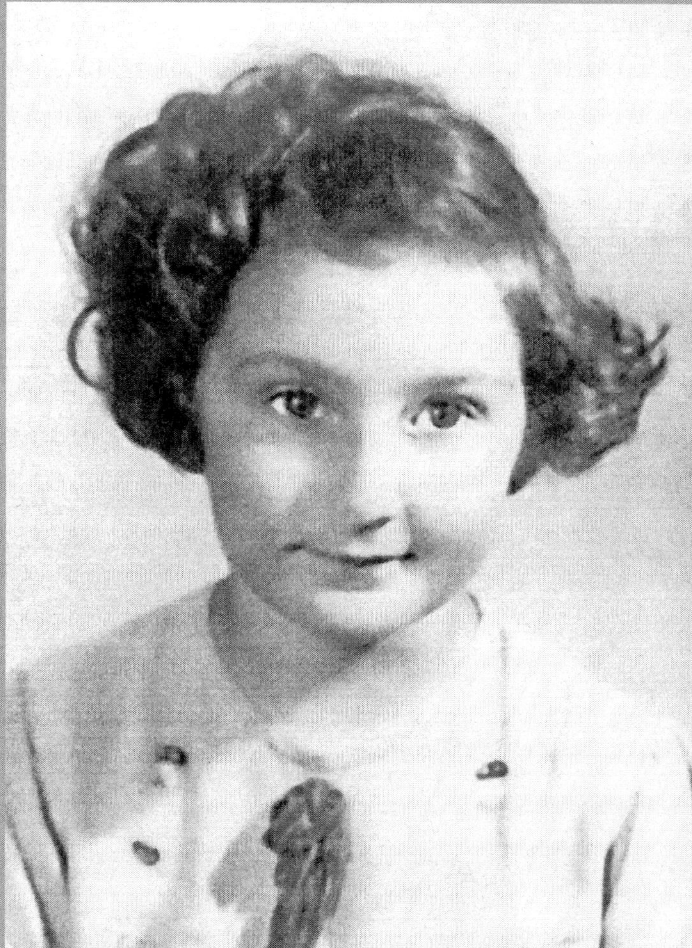

Sharona as a four-year-old. Her parents needed this picture for their application of an exit visa for Palestine.

4. 'See you next year in Jerusalem'

An encounter with a Jewish girl from Lwów

"There are circumstances in which it all comes down to knowledge. If you know, you can act. Not wanting to know is a sin."

Sharona is a powerful presence, somebody who cannot be ignored. Large green eyes peer out earnestly from her round, open face – but also with a touch of humor – into the world. In spite of the shades of gray in her medium-length hair, you mistake her for being younger than her seventy-four years. She immediately figures you out, but she is also friendly. Sharona is a woman of character, somebody you can trust.

She states things plainly in her dark, often rather husky voice. She does not mince her words, sometimes speaking with a serious emphasis, as if to test whether you are aware of the seriousness of life. Sharona has seen the deepest caverns of the human soul. However, she was never a victim. It has only made her stronger.

Sharona Igra was born in Lwów. She witnessed everything. She is married to another "survivor," Itzchak Komem. He was born in the Polish city of Kalisz and survived the Holocaust in hiding as a child in Warsaw. The couple live in Jerusalem. Sharona is a clinical psychologist and remains active in her profession.*

For more than one reason, it is a miracle that we can speak with her. This is the third and, presumably, last time that Sharona visits her native city. She is only in Lviv for a few days, because her husband Itzchak is one of the speakers at a conference on the Righteous among the Nations. The last time that she returned to Lviv was right after Ukrainian independence. "That was a very emotional visit. For the first time, I again saw the house where I was born and where I experienced all of my earliest memories. Everything was still there, but the drab haze of communism was hanging over the city." Now, she can also enjoy a bit of the warm springtime weather and the busy terraces. Together with her husband, she is visiting the places that are connected to her family history.

---

* In December 2014 Itzchak Komem passed away at the age of nearly 80 years.

Sharona's first memories are ink-black and blood-red. She was four years old when the German army came marching into Lwów. A few days afterward, the first pogrom broke out. Under the supervising eye of the Germans, Ukrainians and Poles indiscriminately hunted Jews. Their hatred was vented in an unrestrained and chaotic way. "Never had I seen so much blood," Sharona remembers. After that, the more organized raids, the Aktionen, followed. The first one, in the springtime of 1942, had been directed against "anti-social elements" – children and old people who could not work.

The raids are a clear memory in Sharona's mind. The Igra family lived at 5 Gazova Street. During the first big Aktion, the family hid in a factory in Słoneczna Street (now Kulisha Street). After three long days, the situation there became unbearable, so they decided to return home. A Ukrainian man who lived across from them quickly pulled Sharona inside his house and told her parents that it was much too dangerous for children – the raid was still going on. That day, many children were picked up. She has never known the name of that neighbor, but his act still fills her with gratitude.

Later, during the same Aktion, Sharona's grandmother was arrested and murdered on the spot; it happened in their staircase. Sharona had been hidden away under a bedspread. She can still hear her grandmother's last cry and the blows of her skull against the steps when they dragged her downstairs.

A few weeks later, when there were German officers in their house, her mother hid her in an enclosed, hollow space under the table. She remembers that her parents spoke to them; her parents had arrived as refugees in Prague and Vienna during World War I and had learned German there. She was not discovered. "I learned fast in those days. I understood at an early age what death meant. Every week, we heard whispering about relatives who had been 'taken away'. I understood that they would never come back again."

She remembers Ukrainian boys on her block who would wait for her and chase her. "They called me names, like "zydóweczka" ["little Jew" – derogative word in Polish]. I was so afraid of those boys."

Sharona's father decided to clutch at a final straw. There was a call to Jews with identity documents for British Palestine to report to the Gestapo. The Germans wanted to exchange them for the German Templars who had been detained by the British in Palestine. They were promised that not a hair on their heads would be harmed. They would receive a certificate that would prove that they were residents of Palestine.

Sharona's parents had the correct papers at their disposal because they were Zionists. "Whether or not it was a trap was unclear. But father said: 'I have had enough of hiding and being hunted as prey. We would be better off in the mouth of the lion.'"

With several hundred other people, the family was locked up in a large building on what is now Stepan Bandera Street (at number 49). "For me, this street is still Leona Sapiehy Street; Bandera is, especially for Jews, a controversial name. I remember the building well. There was a spacious courtyard, where we could play freely. We were treated relatively well. At that moment, they would have nothing if we were to perish," Sharona says cynically.

Nevertheless, after three months, they were dispatched to the Bergen-Belsen concentration camp. There, they were detained as hostages in a Sonderlager (special camp). Up to that point, only military personnel had been detained there, as Soviet prisoners of war. Sharona's was the first group of ordinary citizens to arrive in Bergen-Belsen. They were people with foreign passports, from various countries.

Sharona remembers how extremely hungry she was in the camp: "Somebody who has never experienced that cannot imagine how it feels; I cannot describe it. We were as thin as skeletons." Between their section and the rest of the camp were high fences with barbed wire, with no-man's land in between. Sometimes, things were thrown over the fence. She remembers that Dutch women arrived from the Ravensbrück concentration camp. They had apparently been deported only recently. The Dutch women threw medicines to them; as a result, Sharona's mother just barely survived typhoid fever.

How do you retain your humanity in an environment of barbed wire, fences and over-crowded barracks? It is the common thread in Sharona's story. A few meager possessions provided an important foot-hold. Her mother had brought along a few photos and an invitation to her wedding. Three Hebrew books were meaningful: *The Song of Solomon*, a gift from her husband, a *Haggadah* printed in Lwów in 1930 and the Hebrew alphabet, from which the children were taught from time to time, for better or for worse.

"Everything was done in the greatest secrecy. We even celebrated our holidays, if that was possible. A gifted young woman rehearsed children's plays with us to perform at Chanukah and Purim. We had Pesach twice in Bergen-Belsen, 'thanks' to the Germans."

"There were readings from the Haggadah. People sat on top of the plank bunks, which were pulled together in the barracks. There were always people on guard, because the celebration was strictly forbidden. We read the story of the deliverance.

"A rabbi who was ill and very emaciated conducted the observance. The man had lost his wife and daughter. I remember how he cried while reading the last pages: 'This year we are slaves, but next year we will be free people.' His voice faltered many times during the narration, but at the end of the Haggadah, he said in a firm voice: 'See you next year in Jerusalem!'"

"We looked at the marvelous illustrations in the Haggadah. There was a picture of rabbis who looked well and healthy, sitting at a table abundantly covered with food. It was as if we, famished children, were looking at an alien world."

Other aspects of life had to continue, as well. Sharona remembers a man who had stolen bread – a mortal sin amongst so much hunger. The people were furious and wanted to beat him up on the spot. However, Sharona's father urged them to stay calm, saying, "This man was perhaps not bad, but was so hungry that he could not do otherwise. Let us take the matter to court." There was a prosecutor, a lawyer and a judge. The "trial" lasted from morning till evening. Sharona no longer remembers the verdict, but it depicts how the prisoners did not want to lose their human dignity.

People preserve the dignity of the human spirit by keeping their lives human – by continuing to live their own lives as much as possible. Religious and cultural traditions helped them to survive.

Sharona reveals, "We lived in the most horrible circumstances. Every day we had to deal with hunger, misery, illness and filth. The contrast was great when, on the first Jewish New Year in the camp, in the fall of 1943, the prayer *Avinu Malkeinu* was sung in harmony by three young women sitting on their plank bunks. My mother sang as well. That was so beautiful."

They saw corpses lying throughout the camp in the last months; the crematorium could no longer cope with the number of dead.

Sharona and her parents endured until April of 1945. One week before Bergen-Belsen would be liberated by the British, their group was placed on a train. The train was bombed several times along the way. Ultimately, it was the Americans who liberated them in the village of Hillersleben, near Magdeburg.

There they were housed for a short time; the locals had to make space for them. Sharona's father and the other leaders of the group managed to go with an American army vehicle that took the orphans from Bergen-Belsen to Paris. On the way, they also collected and took along orphans from Buchenwald. The women and the other children stayed behind, waiting for the Palestine certificates. Then the red Soviet flag appeared in Hillersleben. Sharona's mother wanted to leave before the Soviets arrived. She said that she had not survived Bergen-Belsen for two years only to submit to the yoke of the Soviets. The women took the initiative and made sure that the entire group was able to leave on a train.

Sharona remembers how their train passed the German-Dutch border. It was after midnight on her birthday, 23 June 1945. Hungry Dutch mothers and children crowded together around the train and begged for food. The camp women distributed the food they had received from the Americans. With the rest of the food, they bribed the engineer so that he would continue on to Belgium. At long last, they traveled by ship with the first legal group from France to Palestine. On Rosh Hashanah, 8 September 1945, they arrived in Palestine. There, her parents chose to speak only Hebrew. Sharona forgot how to speak the Polish of her childhood; later, she had to re-learn it.

She still has the books that were so essential to their mental and emotional survival. These are Sharona's documents of her childhood days in Lwów. "Now, we read with the family from the same Haggadah at home on Passover Seder, with our children and grandchildren. The grandchildren know that this is the Haggadah that their great-grandparents took with them from Lwów, which went from Lwów to Bergen-Belsen, and from Bergen-Belsen to Hillersleben to Paris, and finally ended up in Jerusalem."

Itzchak and Sharona were married in Israel by Rabbi Dr. David Kahane, the famous rabbi who had endured the war thanks to Metropolitan Archbishop Andrey Sheptytsky, who had helped him go into hiding in his residence. Kahane wrote a diary during the war that became well-known and was published in Hebrew, Polish, English and Ukrainian.

Sharona also worked for three years on a voluminous book, in which she processed all of her memories, feelings and ideas. It is full of illustrations and documents. Passing on the story is essential to her. She refers to the Haggadah, which means "narrative".

The Haggadah contains the commandment: tell it to your son "... We must pass on the story of the liberation to the children, the grandchildren, to the next generation ... until the very last generation. I dedicated the book to my children and grandchildren, and to the grandchildren and great-grandchildren who have not yet been born, but who might perhaps read this book over the course of time."

However, the book is not for publication. Sharona does not wish to flaunt her Holocaust experience. We leaf through it. We see pictures of her family: her grandmother, her father in the photo that had to be made for the German Ausweis (identity card), a photo of Sharona as a child. The book also contains a picture of an Arbeitsausweis (work permit) and documents which state that they are citizens of Palestine. We also see photos of her father with a hollow, sunken face after being liberated from Bergen-Belsen.

"I wanted to express my individuality and the individuality of my family through this book. To tell our own story, as opposed to the way Israel deals with the Holocaust. The victims are seen as a collectively humiliated people. But every story is different. Everyone experienced it differently and came out differently. We have to acknowledge that plurality and should not attempt to present just one story."

The lesson from Sharona is that "knowing" is important. "After the liberation, there were these blond Aryan women in Germany who said that they did not know anything. In such horrendous times, many people remain spectators and do nothing. Knowing is a moral obligation. The man who pulled me inside his house during the Aktion knew what was going on and also what he had to do. In a fraction of a second, he made the correct decision – he wanted this child to live. There are circumstances in which it all comes down to knowledge. If you know, you can act. Not wanting to know is a sin."

During her short visit to Lviv, Sharona accepted our invitation to speak before an audience of Ukrainian students from the Catholic University. Her opening question for the students was: "Do your grandparents ever tell you anything about World War II and, if so, what do they tell you?"

The students are impressed by her story. Not only is it the first time that they hear an eyewitness speak about the Holocaust, but it is also the first time that they hear unambiguous stories about the atrocities that were committed by Ukrainians. Sharona clarifies, however, that she does not blame this third generation in any way. Her commitment is focusing on the future.

A Palestinian illustrator also contributed to her book. As a psychologist in Israel, Sharona is a member of "Psychoactive," part of the Mental Health Professionals for Human Rights. Therewith, she undertakes activities that promote human rights, including issues concerning Palestinians under occupation.

Places of the Holocaust

The memories from Sharona Igra's childhood are gruesome. However, hers is also a story of great strength of mind and courage. It leads us directly into the atrocities of the persecution of the Jews during World War II. In the previous chapters, the Holocaust has been present as a dark background that marked this city and its people. It is an unfathomably deep ravine, into which many residents of Lviv do not dare to look. Erasing almost all Jewish inhabitants, followed by the expulsion of the German and Polish population from the city, marked an irreparable fracture between the pre- and post-war history of Lviv. After that, absolutely everything would be different.

At which locations did the horrors of the Holocaust play out? How did it begin in Lwów? What was the role and the attitude of the rest of the population towards the Jews, and that of the church? What can the visitor of today see or find of these places of bitter memories?

The ghetto

The house in which Sharona lived, on Gazova Street, was close to the entrance of the former Jewish ghetto. That entrance was formed by the "Gate of Death," which is how the railroad viaduct over Prospekt Chornovola was known. The ghetto was north of the railroad. At first, it extended to both sides of Prospekt Chornovola, but as a result of the deportations and mass executions, the ghetto soon shrank to a smaller area at the eastern side of the Prospekt. As of December, 1941, the Jews of Lwów were forced to live here. A second entrance to the ghetto was through the railroad viaduct over Zamarstynivska Street, a little over a hundred yards to the east.

Jewish shop in the Lemberik Ghetto

Those who entered this gate were almost certain that they would meet their end. The Jews tried desperately to find work, as they would receive an Arbeitsausweis that would buy them some time. Sharona's father had such an Ausweis. She saved it and printed it in her book. The column of workers went daily through the gate, always afraid of the arbitrariness and cruelty of the guards.

When you were finally conveyed through the gate to the outside, you knew the end was near – in the Janowska labor camp, on the sandy soils

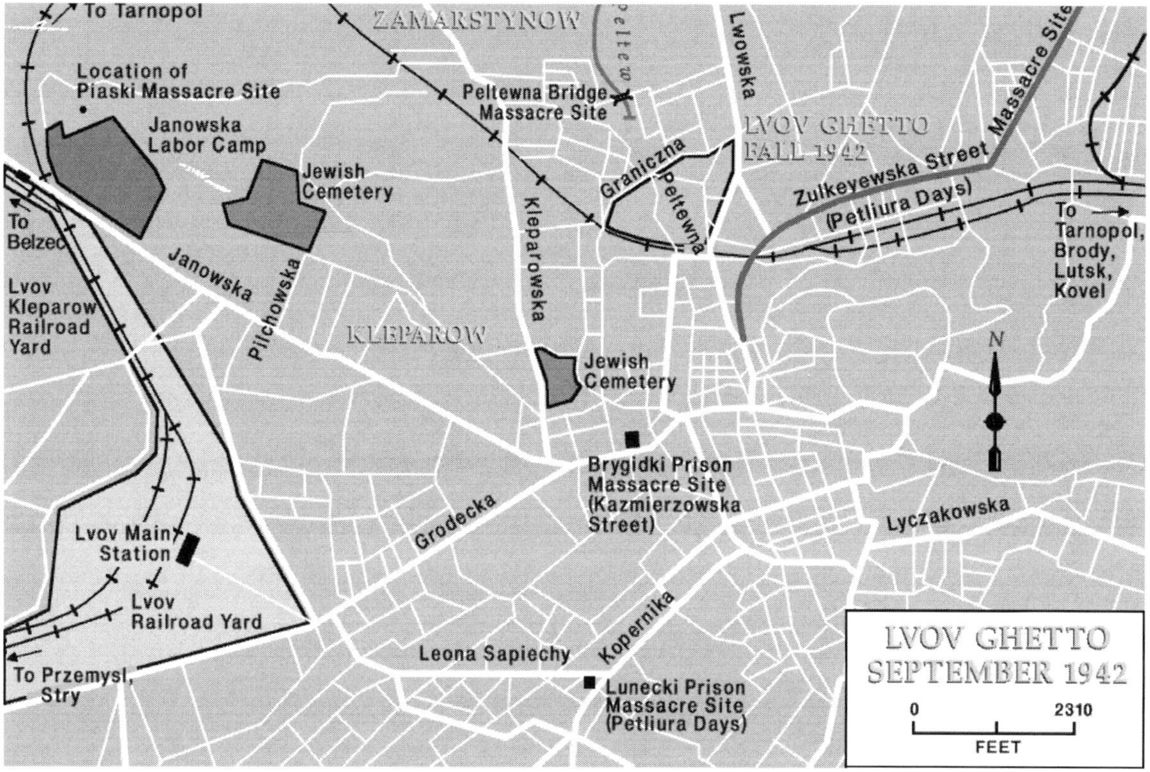

(*Piaski* in Polish, *Pisky* in Ukrainian) behind it or in the Bełzec extermination camp, about one hour by train from Lwów. When nearly all of the people were gone (dead or deported), the ghetto was burned down on 1 June 1943. Contrary to information from several sources, the fire did not raze everything to the ground; many buildings and residential blocks from that era are still standing.

Immediately after the overpass on the Prospekt, on the right, is the ghetto monument to the 136,000 victims of the Lviv Ghetto. It was erected in 1992. The Sholem Aleichem Jewish Culture Society raised the money for it. In the foreground is a menorah, the candelabra with seven arms, with a large, abstract sculpture of a human figure behind it, surrounded by tall trees. Until 1992, there were no memorials for the deported Jews of Lwów.

Olga Shyrokova (see chapter 3) says of this monument: "I like the gesture of the figure that has been portrayed. He utters a loud cry of despair up to the sky. All the horror is contained in that cry – all of the atrocities that were committed against the Jews in Lviv. At the same time, he has his right hand open – he still expects all of God's help."

The Ukrainian text below the menorah says: "Remember and keep it in your heart." At the right side of the path that leads to the statue are private memorial stones. These were purchased and placed here by relatives of people who were murdered, either at this site or elsewhere.

The devastated Great Suburban Synagogue

The Brygidky Prison on Horodotska Street

Persecution of the Jews in Lwów

The violence against the Jewish community did not just fall from the sky. As in other places in this part of Europe, it was not difficult to stir up existing feelings of resentment. It seemed as if people were just waiting for a provocation. There was already an anti-Semitic tone prevalent in the Polish republic. Since the 1930s, more and more anti-Jewish measures had been taken. The writer Leopold Unger wrote about the climate for Jews in Lwów at the beginning of the 1930s: "The times (and the studying) were not easy. The anti-Semitic campaign in politics was ushered into the city by an economic boycott, through sentries in front of Jewish shops, accompanied by raids from organized gangs. The appearance of a Jew in a hallway or stairwell at the university could end in violence." **(1)**

Around 1939, 110,000 Jews lived in Lviv; that was approximately one-third of its total population. In September of 1939, the Russians occupied the city. This was the result of the Molotov-Ribbentrop Pact, which divided Poland between Germany and the Soviet Union. Many Jews fled the Nazis from the west to Lwów, where they were relatively safe under the Russians. Lwów became a haven for these Jews.

The number of Jewish residents increased to 160,000 within a few months. Under the Soviet regime, they received equal status with other nationalities – this meant an improvement for the Jewish community. The theaters were running full houses, Yiddish newspapers were published and religious life could proceed. Religious leaders were not imprisoned or deported, as had been happening with the priests of the Ukrainian churches.

Some Jews cooperated with the Soviet authorities, but others were persecuted. In April 1940, hundreds of Jews were deported to Siberia when they refused to accept Soviet nationality. Everyone who was suspected of being a nationalist – Polish, Ukrainian or Jewish – faced terror.

The relative safety was short-lived. In June 1941, the Germans attacked the Soviet Union and on the last day of the month, 30 June 1941, they invaded Lwów. Poles and Ukrainians initially welcomed the Germans as liberators: they brought an end to the Stalinist terror.

Pogroms broke out immediately in the city. They were initiated by Ukrainian and Polish anti-Semites, but the Germans helped with their propaganda machine. They blamed the Jews for the mass murder of Ukrainian and Polish nationalists in the Brygidky Prison **(2)** and the prison on Lontskoho Street. **(3)** The NKVD had executed thousands of prisoners shortly before the German invasion, including a large portion of the Ukrainian intelligentsia – teachers, doctors, lawyers and writers. The courtyards were full of corpses. Through pamphlets and extensive footage on the Deutsche Wochenschau, the German newsreel, the Nazis fanned the flames: the treacherous Jews were to blame for these crimes. The propaganda fit perfectly with the image that many people already had, one where communists and Jews were accomplices.

Monument to the victims at the entrance of the ghetto

This viaduct was at a distance of about 110 yards from a similar overpass, which was the entrance to the ghetto: the "Gate of Death."

About two thousand Jews were murdered in the streets of Lwów during the first pogrom. People were hunted down, locked in the prison yards and brutally beaten. Women were dragged naked through the streets. This is the pogrom to which Sharona refers in her story. Never in her life had she seen as much blood as on that day. A short time later, the Jews were forced to wear a Star of David, a white band with a blue star. Another pogrom followed. At the same time, the Germans began to systematically destroy the synagogues and cemeteries of the city.

In July 1941, the Judenrat (Jewish Council) was established, which was primarily intended to recruit a Jewish workforce. The first chairman was the lawyer Dr. Joseph Parnes; however, he was executed in November because he refused to carry out German orders. His successor was Henryk Landsberg. The Judenrat tried to remain in charge in spite of the difficult circumstances. For instance, it organized the police who controlled life in the ghetto.

In October, the first Jews were recruited to build a labor camp in Janowska Street. It was to become a notorious concentration camp where people died of starvation, disease, exhaustion and torture.

The order to set up a ghetto north of the railroad followed in November. Before the fifteenth of December, all Jews were forced to move there. Soon, around 120,000 Jews lived in the ghetto. The first deportations from the ghetto to the Belzec extermination camp began in March 1942. They were transported from the Klepariv railway station – close to the Janowska camp – in cattle cars. From June of 1942, the mass executions took place on the sandy soils (Pisky or Piaski) near the camp. There was also a mass execution site in the forest of Lysynychi, at the eastern edge of Lwów.

In addition to large-scale deportations to concentration camps, many Jews in Galicia and eastern Poland were liquidated in another way. They were murdered by bullets – often near their own city or village – after having been forced to dig their own graves. The French researcher Patrick Desbois called this mass murder of the Jews of Eastern Europe a "Holocaust by bullets." **(4)**

The wall of the Janowska camp still exists

After the raid that took place during the massive August Action, by that same month of 1942, about 65,000 Jews were left. The conditions in the ghetto were extremely primitive. There was a lack of water, food and medicine, and it was overcrowded. People even lived in holes in the ground. The executions on the sandy soils continued, with tens of thousands being murdered every month.

On 1 September 1942, the Gestapo publicly hanged all the members of the Judenrat from a balcony in the ghetto; they were no longer needed. On the first of June 1943, the liquidation of the ghetto took place. Houses were blown up with explosives or set on fire. The last Jews were executed on 18 November 1943. In less than two and a half years, about 200,000 Jews had been annihilated. Reportedly, only 832 Jews who had hidden in monasteries or private dwellings survived in Lwów. This was the official count when the Red Army seized the city on 18 July 1944.

Siman Wiesenthal (1908-2005)

The Janowska concentration camp (5)

It is perplexing that the Janowska concentration camp still exists in its original state – and not as a museum or memorial, but as a prison that is still in full operation. When the Soviet troops arrived in 1944, they took over the camp and designated it as a prison for criminals and political prisoners. It is now a Ukrainian state prison.

The complex offers a lurid and gruesome sight: many walls surrounded by barbed wire, and also a few watchtowers. There are no signs that explain what this is – or was. Dilapidated, dark-red brick buildings with a factory chimney are visible on the grounds of the prison. These were the factory buildings of D.A.W. (Deutsche Ausrüstungswerke), a company of the SS that manufactured army equipment. The production buildings also stood in the vast environs of the camp. You can walk along the wall, parallel to the busy highway known as Shevchenka Street, which then turns into Vinnytsya Street. Keep to the wall at your right. A little further along, there is an unpaved path. The brick walls you walk next to were built by the first Jewish forced laborers. Beware of taking pictures: a maximum-security prison falls under "Objects of the State" and you will be closely monitored from the watchtower.

Behind the Janowska camp were the sandy soils where tens of thousands of people were executed and buried in mass graves, then dug up again by camp inmates. The bodies were burned and pulverized, and the ash and skeletal remains were scattered over the grounds.

Leon Wells **(6)** (Polish name: Wieliczker) belonged to the Sonderkommando, the "special units" responsible for burning the corpses. He wrote an impressive book about his years in the Janowska camp and was a witness at the trial of Adolf Eichmann. Simon Wiesenthal **(7)**, who dedicated his life to the prosecution of Nazi criminals, was also a survivor of the Janowska camp. He had to repair railway parts in the camp.

Pogrom

Janowska Memorial (8)

A stone was erected in 1993 at the entrance to the Piaski, with an inscription that reads: "Let the memory of all the genocide victims in the Janowska death camp remain forever, 1941-1943" (also in Hebrew and Ukrainian). Among the 200,000 murdered people that are commemorated, the victims of other mass execution sites in Lviv are included. The Alexander Schwarz International Holocaust Center is committed to ensuring that there will be a more worthy memorial to the murdered victims, most of whom were Jewish.

You arrive at the former sand hills through an opening in an iron partition. This terrain was, until about ten years ago, used to train police dogs. It is now a grassy area with an elongated pool along the left-hand side. The spot is called the Babi Yar of Lviv, after the ravine where the Jews of Kyiv met their end on 29 and 30 September 1941. It is a quiet place. The earth here is mixed with blood and human remains. An endless dirge murmurs through the trees.

The deportations to Bełzec took place at the Kleparow station, which is several hundred yards from the Janowska camp. A modest commemorative plaque can be seen there. **(9)**

The story of Rabbi David Kahane and Metropolitan Sheptytsky

It is an extraordinary coincidence. Sharona tells us that she and Itzchak had been married by Rabbi David Kahane. Just like Sharona, Rabbi Kahane was a survivor of the Holocaust in Lwów. They did not know it then; they chose him because he spoke Polish.

Two locations in Lviv are connected with Rabbi Kahane. First of all, there is the spot where his synagogue stood at Bankivska Street. **(10)** It was one of the places where the progressive community met. Nowadays, you stumble again into such a characteristically empty area. The synagogue must have stood behind the present garbage dump in the middle of the street.

The second place is the Saint George Cathedral (Sobor Sviatoho Yura), at the end of Lystopadovoho Chynu Street. From many places in the town center, it is possible to see the mighty Baroque dome rising in the distance. In the adjacent palace of Metropolitan Archbishop Andrey Sheptytsky (1865-1944; leader of the Ukrainian Greek Catholic Church), David Kahane was in hiding during the war. He wrote about it in his diary, which was published in English in 1972 as *Lvov Ghetto Diary*.

Andrey Sheptytsky (1865-1944)

The Greek Catholic Church, to which the vast majority of the Ukrainian population of the city belonged, had suffered tremendously during the Soviet terror of 1939–1941. The church and its leaders perceived the arrival of the Germans as a liberation and hoped that the ideal of an independent Ukrainian state could finally be achieved.

When the bloody pogroms against the Jews broke out immediately after the German invasion – with Ukrainian nationalists in the lead – Rabbi Lewin of the Progressive Tempel Synagogue went to Metropolitan Archbishop Sheptytsky in his residence near the Saint George Cathedral. He informed him about the massacres and begged him to use his prestige to intervene with the German authorities. In response to the rabbi's plea for help Sheptytsky issued his pastoral letter of 1 July 1941 in which he called on the Ukrainian government that had been proclaimed the previous day to respect the rights of all citizens. According to Kurt Lewin, Rabbi Lewin's son who survived the war in hiding in Sheptytsky's residence, the Metropolitan also instructed his priests and monks to go out into the streets and try to stop the violence.

The Metropolitan also offered Rabbi Lewin a hiding place within his palace. The rabbi refused. He said that his place was with his community and left to return home. Later that day, his body was found; he had been taken to the prison by Ukrainian policemen, but it was men in German uniforms who shot him. This happened in the Brygidky prison, the same prison where just a few days earlier the NKVD had shot the political prisoners in large numbers right before the arrival of the Germans, amongst whom were many leaders of the Ukrainian national movement.

At the beginning of the German occupation, Metropolitan Sheptytsky was more concerned with moderating the nationalists than standing up for the Jews. He was, for instance, opposed to the greeting Slava Ukraini! ("Glory to Ukraine!"), with which Stepan Bandera's supporters had replaced the traditional greeting of "Glory to Jesus Christ!"

However, from February 1942 onwards, in pastoral letters, the Metropolitan began to vigorously condemn the mass murder of the Jews that was occurring in the cities and villages of Galicia. His letters followed the terrorist attacks and raids that took place in the ghetto of Lwów. One of his most famous pastoral letters is from 21 November 1942, titled "Thou shalt not kill." The Metropolitan condemned any murder of a fellow human being as a grave sin. He realized that, among his believers, there were many who had blood on their hands. He called upon young people not to sign up for the Ukrainian police, which assisted the Germans in hunting down and killing Jews. Christians had to show love for their neighbors and be prepared to sacrifice themselves for their fellow men. The Metropolitan slowly shifted towards the viewpoint that the Nazis were worse than the Bolsheviks.

Commemoration place on the grounds of the former Janowska camp

In 1943, German officials asked Metropolitan Sheptytsky to support the establishment of a Ukrainian division of the Waffen SS, known as the SS Division Galicia. The Metropolitan refused to give his support and agreed only to provide chaplains. In Galicia, young men were encouraged to apply as volunteers. Coadjutor Archbishop Josyf Slipyj, the future Metropolitan of the Greek Catholic Church, held a mass for the recruits. It may be that Sheptytsky's decision for pastoral support was motivated by his preference for a regular Ukrainian army over wayward gangs. If a transition to an independent Ukrainian state were to occur, a professional army would protect the populace from chaos and anarchy.

Thus, it is not a straightforward story about Metropolitan Sheptytsky. But it should be said that he had personally devoted himself to rescuing Jews. He gave shelter to Rabbi Kahane after May 1943, when the ghetto had been liquidated. He ensured that the sons of the murdered Rabbi Lewin, Kurt (Isaac) and Nathan, could go into hiding in Greek Catholic monasteries and in his own residence at the Saint George Cathedral. He provided false baptismal certificates, so that Jewish children had protection. He was directly responsible for saving the lives of a total of one hundred fifty Jews, mostly children.

The State of Israel has not posthumously awarded Metropolitan Sheptytsky the accolade of Righteous among the Nations, as Jewish survivors have urged. His role is too ambiguous, too controversial. Historical research into this highly complex and painful episode in the history of the Ukrainian nation is still ongoing. **(11)**

Dealing with memories, places of new life

There are a few modest Holocaust memorials in Lviv, but there is still no worthy museum dedicated to the Jewish history of the city and the destruction of the Jewish population. We would like to continue this chapter by acknowledging a few less visible activities, which nonetheless demonstrate that the interest in the Jewish history of Lviv is growing – not only among the Jewish community, but also among newer generations of Ukrainian people. There are some hopeful signs of attempts at rapprochement and collaboration towards a multicolored culture of remembrance, of Ukrainians, Poles, Jews, Armenians and Germans.

Museum room

A real museum is not yet there, but rather a "museum room." It is located in the building of the All-Ukrainian Charitable Foundation Hesed-Arieh, on Kotlyarevskoho Street. **(12)** The little museum has a permanent exhibition called *Tracing Galician Jews*. There is a collection of objects and photographs that show how rich and diverse the contribution of Jews was to the economic, social, cultural and religious life of the city. Naturally, there is also one wall dedicated to the Shoah. You can buy recordings of old and new Yiddish music and books on the Jewish history of Lviv. Hesed-Arieh is also dedicated to cultural activities, such as the annual Jewish culture festival, and offers courses and lectures.

The American Jewish Joint Distribution Committee is housed in the same building on Kotlyarevskoho Street. This organization provides social assistance to indigent, elderly and sick people. On the Sabbath, the liberal Jewish congregation of Rabbi Siva Fainerman meets here.

Center for Urban History

The Center for Urban History of East Central Europe gives important impetus for the study of Jewish life in Lviv and for the conservation of the remains of cultural heritage. It was founded in 2004 through a private initiative. The center offers information and documentation and enables much of it to be accessible on the Internet. **(13)** Director Sofia Dyak represents an expert and calming voice when feelings are running high in the public debate involving Jewish sites in Lviv. In conjunction with the Center for Urban History, the Lviv City Council has organized a competition for architects: how shall we preserve the Jewish memorial places and how can they be filled with new life?

Universities

Nowadays, the universities in Lviv are more frequently organizing conferences and seminars dealing with the Jewish past, including the Holocaust. We met Sharona and Itzchak Komem at one of these conferences. The Ukrainian Catholic University initiated a collaborative program with the Hebrew University of Jerusalem. Together, they do research on the Jewish history of Galicia and Bukovina. At the heart of the project is the creation of a comprehensive electronic database of source material on Judaism in Galicia and Bukovina. In this way, the universities continue the tradition of a famous citizen of Lwów whose name is remembered by, unfortunately, few people: Raphael Lemkin (1900-1959). He studied law at the University of Lwów. He was of Jewish descent, was able to escape to Sweden in 1941 and went from there to the United States. Lemkin was the father of the concept of "genocide." He used this word for the first time in 1944 in a book in which he described the mass murder of the Jews in Europe as the "systematic and planned destruction of a population." He was a legal adviser at the Nuremberg Tribunal and was the designer of the United Nations Convention on the Prevention and Punishment of the Crime of Genocide, which was adopted in 1948.

Churches

For several years now, the Justice and Peace Commission of the Ukrainian Greek Catholic Church has organized ecumenical prayer services on Victory Day, the ninth of May – the end of World War II – at the monument of the Janowska camp and at sites where other war victims (Jews, Ukrainians, Poles, Germans, Armenians, etc.) are buried. Representatives participate on behalf of the churches and the Jewish community.

Future

The most hopeful sign of a future for Jews in Lviv is perhaps the fact that a few Ukrainian students are learning Yiddish. These young women and men are looking for a bridge to the past, out of great historical interest, in order to seek from that past new and peaceful possibilities of coexistence for today and tomorrow. They pose questions to their parents, their grandparents, to people who were taught to stay silent for half a century. They want to know. They want to listen. And they learn the language that over centuries held Jewish life together: Yiddish. They cannot come any closer. They learn the language of the heart. Their teacher is Boris Dorfman. And so, the circle is completed. In other words, a web of reconciliation is woven over ravines of pain – "Dos lebn setzt sich fort waiter."

Notes

(1) From: Leopold Unger, *Intruz* (Intruder), 2001, a quote from Jean-Paul Hinrichs's book *Lemberg – Lwów – Lviv*, Bas Lubberhuizen, 2008.

(2) The massive Brygidki building at 18 to 20 Horodotska Street dates back to 1614. Formerly the Bridgettine Convent, it became a prison in 1782. Until the 1980s, death penalties were carried out there.

(3) This former prison stands on Briulova Street, which was formerly called Lontskoho Street. There is a museum in memory of the murder of Ukrainian patriots in 1941 and also of the era after World War II, when it was a KGB prison. The name of the museum is *Tyurma na Lontskoho*; it is open from two until six o'clock on Thursday afternoons. Admission is free.

(4) Patrick Desbois, *The Holocaust by Bullets: A Priest's Journey to Uncover the Truth Behind the Murder of 1.5 Million Jews*, (New York: Palgrave-Macmillan, 2008).

(5) The former Janowska camp is located on Shevchenka Street, past the Yanivske cemetery on the right. Route: Take tram 7 at the book market on Pidvalna Street, following the long Shevchenka Street (formerly called Janowska Street) all the way to the end of line 7. Disembark at the end point. Then, walk straight on, parallel to the road (Shevchenka Street turns right here and changes into Vynnytsya Street). There will be an access road to the entrance of the prison, marked by a sign of the Ukrainian state. To the right is the beginning of a long wall covered with graffiti. Behind this wall was the former concentration camp.

(6) Leon (Wieliczker) Wells, *The Death Brigade* (The Janowska Road) (New York: Holocaust Library, 1978).

(7) Simon Wiesenthal, *The Sunflower: On the Possibilities and Limits of Forgiveness* (New York: Schocken Books, 1997).

(8) Walking route, from the endpoint of tramline 7: Walk along the highway, where a partial footpath runs to the memorial. Walk along the wall at your right – this is not the wall of the prison, but rather a second wall that separates the highway from the terrain behind it. After a few hundred yards, you should see the memorial site to your right. It is a large stone with an inscription. Behind the iron doors lies the former execution site. Driving route: Turn right at the end of Shevchenka Street onto Vynnytsya Street; drive a few hundred yards along the wall until you arrive at the inconspicuous turnoff to the memorial place. You can park there.

(9) Turn left at the T-junction on Shevchenka Street; after a few hundred yards, you should arrive at the station, which is now a terminal for the transportation of goods. A memorial plaque is affixed to the wall of the station.

(10) This is now the gaping hole with the garbage dump , recently refreshed by colourful graffiti on the walls, at Bankivska Street (a side-street of Doroshenka Street).

(11) Andrii Krawchuk, *Christian Social Ethics in Ukraine: The Legacy of Andrei Sheptytsky* (Edmonton, Ottawa and Toronto: Canadian Institute of Ukrainian Studies Press, 1997); John-Paul Himka, *Ukrainians, Jews and the Holocaust: Divergent Memories* (Saskatoon: Heritage Press, 2009).

(12) Museum Room Jewish history of Lviv: Tracing Galician Jews. Address: 30 Kotlyarevskoho Street Opening hours: Sunday through Friday from 10:00 a.m. until 5:00 p.m. (Closed on the Sabbath) Admission: Voluntary donation

(13) 6 Akademika Bohomoltsia Street. Website: www.lvivcenter.org/en

Additional readings and films

(in English and German)

Bartov, Omer. *Erased: Vanishing Traces of Jewish Galicia in Present-Day Ukraine*. Princeton: Princeton University Press, 2007.

Berkhoff, C. Karel. *Harvest of Despair: Life and Death in Ukraine under Nazi Rule*. Cambridge: Harvard University Press, 2008.

Biriuliov, Yuriy. *Jewish Heritage of Lviv*. Lviv: Centre of Europe, 2002.

Brandon, Ray; Wendy Lower, eds. *The Shoah in Ukraine: History, Testimony, Memorialization*. Bloomington: Indiana University Press in association with the United States Holocaust Memorial Museum, 2008.

Carynnyk, Marco, "Ministers of Righteousness: Greek Catholic Clergymen and Poles and Jews during the Second World War" (forthcoming article).

De Waal, Edmund. *The Hare with Amber Eyes: A Hidden Inheritance*, Random House UK, 2011.

Desbois, Patrick. *The Holocaust by Bullets: A Priest's Journey to Uncover the Truth Behind the Murder of 1.5 Million Jews*. New York: Palgrave Macmillan, 2008.

Dohrn, Verena. *Reise nach Galizien: Grenzlandschaften des alten Europas*. Frankfurt am Main: S. Fischer Verlag, 1992.

Fässler, Peter, Thomas Held, Dirk Sawitzki. *Lemberg - Lwów – Lviv: Eine Stadt im Schnittpunkt europäischer Kulturen*. Köln, Weimar, Wien: Böhlau Verlag, 1993.

Friedmann, Towiah. *Die Vernichtung der Juden Ost-Galiziens und die Rolle des SS- und Polizeiführers Fritz Katzmann, der die Aktionen in Lemberg und Galizien in den Jahren 1941-1943 leitete*. Haifa: Institute of Documentation in Israel, 2004.

Granach, Alexander. *Da geht ein Mensch: Autobiographischer Roman*. Augsburg: Ölbaum Verlag, 2005.

Granach, Alexander. *From the Shtetl to the Stage: The Odyssey of a Wandering Actor*. New Brunswick, NJ: Transaction Publishers, 2010. (With a new introduction by Herbert S. Lewis.)

Haumann, Heiko. *Geschichte der Ostjuden*. München: Deutsche Taschenbuch Verlag, 1991.

Haumann, Heiko. *A History of East European Jews*. Budapest: Central European University Press, 2002.

Himka, John-Paul. *Ukrainians, Jews and the Holocaust: Divergent Memories*. Saskatoon: Heritage Press, 2009.

Hofbauer, Ernst; Lisa Weidmann, *Verwehte Spuren. Von Lemberg bis Czernowitz: ein Trümmerfeld der Erinnerungen*. Wien: Ibera Verlag, 1999.

Kahane, David. *Lvov Ghetto Diary*. Amherst: University of Massachusetts Press, 1991.

Kessler, Dolph, and Michiel Driebergen, Kees van Ruyven, Ruud Meij. *Lviv, City of Paradoxes*. Mauritsheech Publishers, The Netherlands, and Apriori Publishers, Ukraine, 2014.

Klijanienko, Anna. *Lemberg: Das kulturelle Zentrum der Westukraine*. Berlin: Trescher Verlag, 2008.

Krawchuk, Andrii. *Christian Social Ethics in Ukraine: The Legacy of Andrei Sheptytsky*. Edmonton: Canadian Institute of Ukrainian Studies Press, 1997.

Lehmann, Rosa. *Symbiosis and Ambivalence: Poles and Jews in a Small Galician Town*. New York: Berghahn Books, 2001.

Lemkin, Raphael. *Axis Rule in Occupied Europe. Originally 1944*. Clark: The Lawbook Exchange, 2005. With a new introduction by Samantha Power.

Lyljo, Ihor, and Sorjana Lyljo-Otkowytsch. *Ein Bummel durch die Stadt Lwiw*. Kiew: Baltija Druck, 2005.

Lyljo, Ihor, and Sorjana Lyljo-Otkowytsch. *Touring Lviv*. Kiev: Baltija Print, 2005.

Marshall, Robert. *In the Sewers of Lvov: The Last Sanctuary from the Holocaust*. London: Fontana, 1991.

Melamed, Volodymyr. *The Jews in Lviv (The 13th - First Half of the 20th Century): Events, Society, People*. Lviv, Joint Ukrainian-American Venture Tecor, 1994.

Mendelsohn, Daniel. *The Lost: A Search for Six of Six Million*. New York: HarperCollins, 2006.

Mick, Christoph. "Incompatible Experiences: Poles, Ukrainians and Jews in Lviv under Soviet and German Occupation, 1939-1944," *Journal of Contemporary History 46, 2* (2011): 336-363.

Orach, B.; I. Belous. *Jewish Lviv. One Hundred Addresses*. Tourist map, directory "Hesed-Arieh". Lviv, 2010.

Petrovsky-Shtern, Yohanan, & Antony Polonsky, "Jews and Ukrainians". In: Special issue of *Polin, Studies in Polish Jewry*, Volume 26, Oxford Littman, 2013.

Pollack, Martin. Galizien. *Eine Reise durch die verschwundene Welt Ostgaliziens und der Bukowina.* Frankfurt am Main und Leipzig: Insel Taschenbuch, 2001.

Rosenfeld, Klara. *From Lwów to Parma: A Young Woman's Escape from Nazi-Occupied Poland.* London: Vallentine Mitchell, 2005.

Roth, Joseph. *Werke.* 6 Bände. Köln: Kiepenheuer & Witsch, 1989-1991.

Roth, Joseph. *The Wandering Jews.* London: Granta Books, 2001.

Ruda, Nava. *Zum ewigen Andenken: Erinnerungen eines Mädchens aus dem Ghetto Lwow. Jüdische Familiengeschichte 1899-1999.* Konstanz: Hartung-Gorre Verlag, 2000.

Ruda, Nava. *One day this will be a film: Childhood Memories of a Girl from the Lvov Ghetto.* Nava Ruda's Biography booklet in PDF format can be downloaded or read online: *https://sites.google.com/site/onedaythiswillbeafilm/the-book*

Scheer, Evelyn, and Gert Schmidt. Ukraine. *Zwischen den Karpaten und dem Schwarzen Meer.* Berlin: Trescher-Reihe Reisen, 11. aktualisierte Auflage 2011.

Scheer, Evelyn. *Ukraine-Lesebuch. Literarische Streifzüge durch die Ukraïne.* Berlin: Trescher Verlag, 2006.

Simon, Hermann, Irene Stratenwerth, and Ronald Hinrichs, eds. Lemberg: *Eine Reise nach Europa.* Berlin: Christoph Links Verlag, 2007.

Snyder, Timothy. *Bloodlands: Europe Between Hitler and Stalin.* New York: Basic Books, 2010.

Stanislawski, Michael. *A Murder in Lemberg: Politics, Religion, and Violence in Modern Jewish History.* Princeton: Princeton University Press, 2007.

Stankiewic, Edward. *My War: Memoir of a Young Jewish Poet.* Syracuse: Syracuse University Press, 2002.

Webber, Jonathan (author), Chris Schwarz (photographer). *Rediscovering Traces of Memory: The Jewish Heritage of Polish Galicia.* Bloomington: Indiana University Press, 2009.

Weiss, Jakob. *The Lemberg Mosaic.* New York: Alderbrook Press, 2011.

Wells, Leon Weliczker. *The Death Brigade* (The Janowska Road). New York: Holocaust Library, 1978.

Wiesenthal, Simon. *The Sunflower: On the Possibilities and Limits of Forgiveness.* New York: Schocken, 1998.

Winstone, Martin. *The Holocaust Sites of Europe: An Historical Guide.* London: I.B.Tauris, 2010.

Wolff, Larry. *The Idea of Galicia: History and Fantasy in Habsburg Political Culture.* Stanford: Stanford University Press, 2010.

Wynne, Suzan. *The Galitzianers: The Jews of Galicia, 1772-1918.* Tucson: Wheatmark, 2006.

Yones, Eliyahu. *Die Strasse nach Lemberg: Zwangsarbeit und Widerstand in Ostgalizien 1941-1944.* Frankfurt am Main: Fischer Taschenbuch Verlag, 1999.

Yones, Eliyahu. *Smoke in the Sand: The Jews of Lvov in the War Years 1939-1944.* Jerusalem: Gefen, 2004.

Four recent films

In Darkness (2011)

This movie, made by the famous Polish director Agnieszka Holland, is based on a true story. Leopold Socha, a sewage worker, hides paying Jews in the sewers of the city. The film tells the moving story of individual men, women and children who try to escape their deadly fate. The story was recorded in a book by Robert Marshall, In *the Sewers of Lvov*. The movie received an Oscar nomination for Best Foreign-Language Film in 2011.

Three Stories of Galicia (2010)

This documentary was made by two young women, Olha Onyshko and Sarah Farhat. It is a portrait of three people who are trapped between Hitler and Stalin, trying to do what is right. The film presents three sensitive and controversial themes of World War II in Galicia: the Holocaust, the Ukrainian Resistance Army and the Polish-Ukrainian conflict.

A radically Yiddish Film: Boris Dorfman - A Mentsh (2014)

A documentary film by Uwe and Gabriela von Seltmann, Apfelstrudel Media Berlin.

Shimon's Returns (2015)

This documentary shot in Poland, Ukraine and Israel tells the story of Shimon Redlich, a Holocaust survivor who returns to places from his childhood as well as different hiding places from his struggle to survive. The film features archival footage from the 1948 Yiddish film Unzere Kinder, in which Shimon acted. A collector of memories and a seeker of good will, Shimon takes us on a journey through Poland and Ukraine, uncovering the brighter sides of the darkest of times.

Internet

Facebook:
www.facebook.com/pages/the-jews-of-lemberg
Organization of Lwow origin Jews (Facebook Group)

Ukrainian website about Jewish heritage:
www.jewishheritage.org.ua/en

www.threestoriesofgalicia.com
www.facebook.com/threestoriesofgalicia

Guided tours along Jewish Heritage in Lviv:
lviv.travel/en/index/what_to_do/excursions/tours

Images of the progrom in Lvov 1941:
https://www.youtube.com/watch?v=CV0-qG9Jdug

Short film about Jewish life in Lvov 1939, produced by Itzhak Goskind, from the collection of the Spielberg Jewish Film Archive:
https://www.youtube.com/watch?v=CQVeL-1BbYs

Maps

The maps on the following pages can be used in addition to a regular city map

1 The Opera House.
2 The Magnus department store.
3 Building of the former Jewish Museum currently houses the Alexander Schwarz International Holocaust Center.
4 The Museum of Ethnography and Art Crafts.
5 Lviv Museum of History of Religion.
6 The Sholem Aleichem Jewish Culture Society, former Jakob Glanzer Synagogue (New Chassidic Synagogue).
7 Building of the former Colosseum shopping arcade from the German family, and the famous Colosseum Theatre.
8 Theatre for Children and Youth, former New Jewish Theater.
9 Signs in Hebrew languague, probably painted after the Second World War .
10 Original signs in Hebrew language.
11 Original signs in Hebrew language.
12 Former editorial office of the Yiddish newspaper the 'Neier Morgen'.
13 Former editorial office of the Yiddish newspaper 'The Lemberger Togblatt'.
14 Former editorial office of the Polish-Jewish newspaper Wschód. On the ground floor once was the Jewish pub 'Maxim'.
15 Former entrance to the Golden Rose Synagogue.
16 The Franz Joseph gymnasium on 5 Kniaza Romana Street.
17 Jewish section of the Yanivske cemetary.
18 The empty place of the former Tempel Synagogue.
19 At the entrance of Dim Legend you will find the traces of a mezuzah site.
20 The empty place of the former Golden Rose Synagogue.
21 Former library from the Golden Rose Synagogue.
22 Former ritual bathhouse of The Golden Rose Synagogue.
23 Former hospital of the Golden Rose Synagogue.
24 Commemorative tablet. The empty place of The Great Suburb Synagogue, Torah school and library.
25 Empty place of the synagogue that belonged to the Beth Lechem Society.
26 Empty place of the Chassidic Schleyen Synagogue.
27 The Beis Aharon V'Yisrael Synagogue, the only functioning synagogue of Lviv.
28 The former Jewish hospital.
29 The Brygidky prison, still in use as prison.
30 The empty place from the former progressive synagogue from Rabbi Kahane.
31 The Center for Urban History of East Central Europe.
32 Kotlyarska str. 1. The house where Sholem Aleichem once lived.
33 Doroshenka Street, once particularly Jewish lawyers lived here.
34 Building of B'nai B'rith, the liberal Jewish community of Lviv and the foundation Hesed-Arieh, with a museum room.
35 Memorial Museum 'Prison at Lontskoho Street'.
36 The former Janowska concentration camp, still in use as a prison.
37 The Janowska Memorial.
38 The Klepariv trainstation with commemorative plaque.

37
36
38
17
7
18
28
3
2
1
5
11
8
4
27
31
35
34
N
0 1.000 2.000 3.000 4.000 5.000

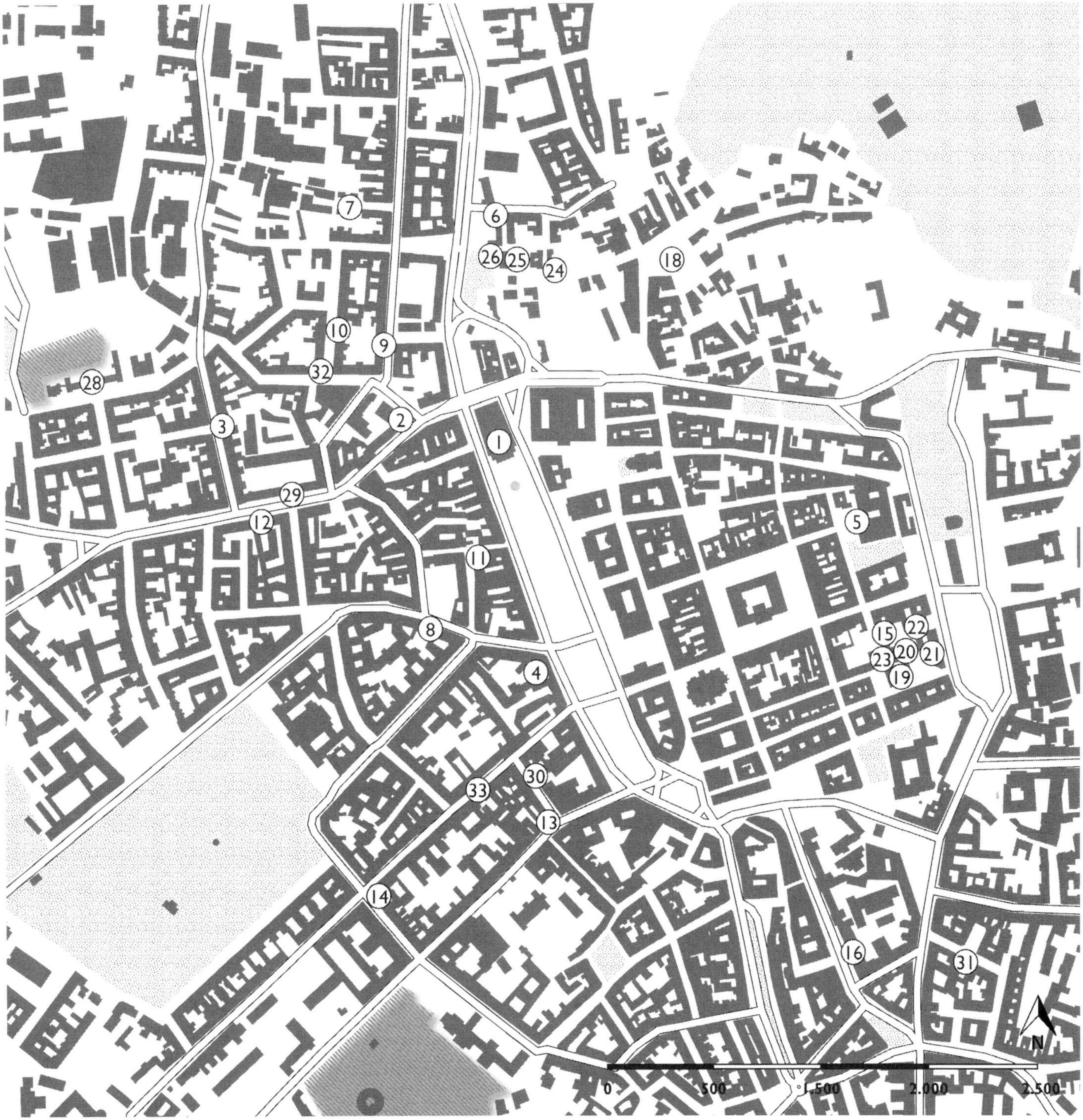

1
2
3
4
5
6
7
8
9
10
11
12
13
14
15
16
18
19
20
21
22
23
24
25
26
28
29
30
31
32
33
N
0
500
1.500
2.000
2.500

Index